St. Lawrence of Brindisi

St. Lawrence Preaching. (*Portrait erroneously attributed to Pietro Labruzzi, now kept in the Capuchin Friary in Florence.*)

St. Lawrence

of Brindisi

by *P. Arturo da Carmignano*
O.F.M.CAP.

Translated by
PAUL BARRETT, O.F.M.CAP.

The Newman Press • *Westminster, Maryland*

1963

Originally published in Rome by Postulazione Generale dei Fratri Minori Cappuccini as *S. Lorenzo da Brindisi.*

Imprimi potest: JACOBUS A. MITCHELSTOWN, O.F.M.CAP.
Min. Prov. Hib.
November 10, 1960

Nihil obstat: JOHN F. DEDE, S.S., J.C.D.
Censor Deputatus

Imprimatur: LAWRENCE J. SHEHAN, D.D.
Archbishop of Baltimore

January 28, 1963

Foreword

THIS BOOK has only one purpose, to provide a quick, simple review of the principal events in the life of St. Lawrence of Brindisi, a great man and a great saint, the greatest man and the greatest saint yet produced by the Capuchin Franciscan Order. A mighty figure as a Superior, orator, warrior, missionary, controversialist and author, St. Lawrence can legitimately take his place among those giants of sanctity, intellect, and action who were raised up for the glory and defense of the Church during the years following the Council of Trent.

The present essay, composed on the occasion of the Saint's being proclaimed a Doctor of the Universal Church, concentrates especially on an examination of his deeds and writings in order to throw into relief his basic characteristics. As the nature of the book demands, we have omitted the usual critical apparatus of scholarship, yet every statement and every conclusion set down here is founded on a diligent and conscientious examination of many documents. In fact, the book is really a brief outline of a three-volume biography of St. Lawrence published recently in Italy and not yet available in English. Meanwhile, we hope that this essay will contribute, however slightly, to the reader's knowledge of a truly great man.

Translator's Acknowledgments

I AM DEEPLY indebted to our revered Minister General, Most Reverend Father Clement of Milwaukee, the present successor of St. Lawrence of Brindisi, for the gracious interest he took in this translation; to Very Reverend Father Hilary, Raheny, Dublin, for comparing the manuscript with the original and for making many valuable suggestions; and to Reverend Father Sylvester, Collegio San Lorenzo, Rome, for his assistance in many ways.

PAUL BARRETT, O.F.M.CAP.

Contents

ONE
The Young Friar   3

TWO
The Preacher   17

THREE
The Superior   37

FOUR
The Warrior   51

FIVE
The Vicar General   71

SIX
The Hammer of Heretics   79

SEVEN
The Ambassador   93

EIGHT
The Peacemaker   111

NINE
The Lover of the Eucharist and of Mary   125

TEN
The Enemy of Oppression   141

ELEVEN
The Doctor of the Church   159

St. Lawrence of Brindisi

Chapter I

The Young Friar

The First Years

ST. LAWRENCE was born at Brindisi in Apulia in southern Italy on July 22, 1559, and was baptized the next day, receiving the name Giulio Cesare. His father, Guglielmo Russo, came from humble stock in Brindisi and, although he had no claim to nobility, he enjoyed an excellent reputation. St. Lawrence's mother, Elisabetta Masella, also came from an unpretentious family in the region.

The home which Divine Providence had prepared for the child was truly worthy of receiving a future saint, for the Russos' deep faith influenced their whole lives and made their little house a haven of peace and harmony. Under the watchful and affectionate eyes of his parents, Giulio grew from infancy to childhood in an atmosphere of joy and love. Although our information about these first years is sparse, we do know of Giulio's prompt obedience to his elders and his popularity with children his own age. We are also able to catch a glimpse of the way in which he, while still a child, was attracted to virtue and to God.

Besides giving evidence that he possessed the highest moral qualities, Giulio showed great intellectual promise. While still very young, he began to attend the day-school conducted by the Conventual Fathers of the

5

monastery of St. Paul where he won his teachers and fellow pupils by his unassuming charm of manner and impressed them with his evident intellectual gifts. It seemed that life offered him only happiness and success, but the outlook soon changed. When he was only about seven or eight years old, death deprived him of his father, who was still a young man. His extremely sensitive soul was deeply wounded by this great loss, yet a supernatural light must have enlightened him and made him feel, at least confusedly, a strong call to a happiness that knows no decline.

"Brother Giulio Cesare"

Some time after his father's death, Giulio asked to be allowed to join the child oblates of the Conventual monastery, where his uncle was a priest. These child oblates were somewhat like our present-day minor seminarians, boys preparing for the life of the cloister by study and recollection under the guidance of an experienced religious. Upon becoming an oblate, Giulio was given a habit similar to that worn by the professed religious and was thenceforth called "Brother Giulio Cesare." The qualities of mind and heart that had already won him the affection and esteem of his young companions soon caught the attention of his new superiors. His teacher was so impressed by his lively intelligence that he had him deliver short sermons in the Cathedral at Brindisi and elsewhere, and the young preacher's fervor and conviction earned him the admiration of his hearers.

In the peace and silence of the cloister, Giulio worked hard at his studies. Soon he was introduced to the ancient classics, which he read with great zest. No doubt it was during this period of his life that he laid the first foundations of that solid classical culture which is evident throughout his later writings. It was also at this time that he began to acquire the familiarity with Latin which was later to permit him to use that language with perfect mastery, great facility, and supreme elegance.

In Venice

Brother Giulio Cesare had been with the Conventual Fathers at St. Paul's for about five years, making daily progress in knowledge, the spiritual life, and union with God, when he experienced a second great sorrow, the death of his mother. Now he was alone, without parents, without a home, and without support, so that he soon was reduced to great need. His poverty and loneliness were not the only trials he had to bear, for about this time he began to experience spiritual distress. He was still very young, just past his childhood, and he found himself confronted by a new world, a world that was more vibrant with life, more alluring and appealing to his emotions than he had found it before. Everything that had hitherto enclosed and satisfied him now gradually lost its charm and attraction, and many things in his new world began to trouble and perplex him.

After much reflection and intense prayer, he resolved to go to Venice to another uncle of his, a priest who was the principal of a private school and who had charge of the clerics at St. Mark's. This uncle received the boy affectionately and was not long in discovering the treasures of grace within his nephew's soul as evidenced by the mystical phenomena which were already

7

to be seen in the youth of less than fifteen years of age. Accordingly, the uncle did not hesitate to set his nephew's feet on the road to sanctity, nor did he delay in fostering the rapid growth of his vocation to the Order of Friars Minor Capuchin.

The Capuchins

On the afternoons of Sundays and feast days, Giulio always went to the small church of St. Mary of the Angels on the island of Giudecca, where the Capuchins used to preach after the singing of Compline. In this way he was able to speak to many of the Friars and become intimately acquainted with the life of these sons of St. Francis. He was so taken with what he saw and heard that after a short time he asked to be allowed to join the order.

Father Lawrence of Bergamo, the Vicar Provincial, received his request favorably and, at the beginning of 1575, sent him to Verona to the novitiate house. On February 18 of the same year, Father Lawrence himself clothed Giulio in the Franciscan habit and, as a sign of special favor, bestowed on him his own name, "Brother Lawrence."

The Young Cleric

The young novice spent his year of probation with great fervor under the direction of holy and enlightened men, and although the precarious state of his health caused some difficulty, he was allowed to make his religious profession on March 24, 1576. At that time, the Constitutions of the Capuchins required that an interval

8

of at least two years should elapse between the end of the novitiate and the resumption of studies. However, an exception was made for Brother Lawrence, so that he was sent at once to Padua to follow the courses in logic and philosophy, and later to Venice for theology.

These five years of study were far from being an easy period for the young cleric. Already during his novitiate year he had suffered from severe pains in the stomach brought on by the austerities and rigors of the Capuchin life. The pains continued during his studies but did not prevent him from adding further penances by denying himself even the necessities of food and sleep.

Unfortunately he soon began to feel the effects of this austerity. His pains increased and his health became so bad that his superiors felt obliged to remove him from studies and send him to the order's infirmary at Oderzo.

With the decline of his health, Brother Lawrence's long-cherished dream of a fervent apostolate seemed to recede further every day. Yet instead of being discouraged he placed himself with childlike faith in the arms of his Heavenly Mother. And she did not fail him, for it was not long before he recovered his health and was able to return to Venice to finish his theological studies.

Studies

At this period, the program of studies in the Province of Venice was already well organized, and in accordance with the admonition of the Constitutions, they were impregnated with "the . . . enkindling charity of Christ, which quickens and humbles the soul." The professors, or lectors, as they were called, did not follow the Thomistic and Dominican tendency by aiming at a cold and, as it were, unfeeling analysis of the truth. Instead, in conformity with the Bonaventurian spirit of their Order, they strove mainly to foster fervor of spirit and a loving knowledge which was intended to lead more to vision and personal experience than to logical truth. The object of the course of studies was, to use the words of St. Bonaventure, "principally fervor and then speculation." This Bonaventurian atmosphere was the best possible climate for encouraging the continued ascent of mind and heart. In it even profane studies became sacred and were transmuted into exercises of virtue, into prayer and acts of love.

As regards method, it seems that the scholastic, speculative mode of teaching had not yet been adopted, the historical, exegetical method being followed instead. That is to say, theology was not first arranged into a system and then studied by the philosophical method. Rather, the student was introduced directly to Sacred Scripture, which he studied with the help of the commentaries written by the Fathers of the Church.

Thus it happened that Brother Lawrence, having brilliantly completed the course in philosophy, was placed in direct contact with Sacred Scriptures in which he studied and deepened his knowledge of Catholic theology. We shall not attempt to describe the joy and satisfaction which he felt upon plunging into that ocean of truth and beauty which we call the Bible. From this point on, the Scriptures became his never-ending study and great love. For the rest of his life, as he travelled about the world, the Bible was to accompany him as a constant and unfailing source of strength and love.

Brother Lawrence's assiduous and loving study was not long in producing its surprising effects. His class-

sium longae finis chartaeque viaeque. $\int$ *E della lunga via BRINDISI il fine*

BRINDISI: CITY AND HARBOR. (*Drawn by S. Pomardi; engraved by P. Parboni. Capuchin Museum, Rome.*)

mates were able to say that he knew the whole Bible by heart and that he was able to give the book, chapter, and verse of any scriptural quotation effortlessly and accurately. Yet this did not satisfy the young cleric. His intuition, his great love and deep respect for the word of God, and a mysterious intimation of his future apostolate led him to embark, almost unaided, on the difficult study of biblical languages. He wished to understand and savor the word of God in its original form, in the very language in which the sacred authors had written it: he wished to taste for himself the full flavor of "Hebrew truth," as he himself called it. He studied Greek and the Aramaic or Chaldaic dialect, as well as Hebrew, and he was so successful, especially in Hebrew,

11

ST. LAWRENCE. (*Engraved by Garofalo Panormitano. Capuchin Museum, Rome.*)

that the rabbis themselves marvelled at his knowledge. But that was not all: he once confided to a friend that, if the whole Bible were lost, he could rewrite it from memory.

Impelled by his ardent desire to penetrate ever more

deeply into the real meaning and mysterious depths of Holy Scripture, he eagerly set about reading and studying the works of the best commentators, both ancient and modern, Christian and Jewish, to the extent that he was convinced that he had read all, or very nearly all, of them.

As can be seen readily, it would be hard to imagine a better and more appropriate preparation for a preacher who was destined one day to confront Protestant theologians, who try to defend their erroneous doctrines by appealing continually to the Bible.

Lenten Preacher

Study, as Brother Lawrence regarded and performed it, could not prevent or even slow down his spiritual development. On the contrary, his studies helped him to climb constantly higher toward the peaks of virtue, toward God. It is our opinion that even Lawrence himself did not know exactly where his study ended and his prayer began because, for him, there could be no dissociation of the one from the other. In fact, one of his colleagues was able to say truly that "he seemed more to pray than to study."

Lawrence's great love for study and his exceptional spiritual fervor gave him a clearly defined and eagerly desired goal, the apostolate of the spoken word, or preaching. He had never forgotten his first informal sermons given in the Cathedral at Brindisi, and during the intervening years he had been looking forward eagerly to the moment when he would again mount the steps of the pulpit. This was the reason why, while still a novice, he had taken the trouble to write down from memory every

13

word of a sermon which he had heard a Dominican preach.

But now the longed-for goal was rapidly drawing near. He had received the tonsure and the four minor orders on September 21, 1577. On December 23, 1581 he received the subdiaconate and soon after he was ordained a deacon. He was still quite young, only twenty-two and a half; nevertheless, he had finished the course of theology and had received his patents to preach. Accordingly, although he was not yet a priest, his superiors decided to entrust him with a very important preaching engagement, the daily Lenten sermon in the parish church of San Giovanni Nuovo in the center of Venice.

Lawrence did not betray the hopes of his superiors and the faithful of the city. The topics he dealt with and the fervor with which he preached won such admiration and so touched the people's hearts that he was immediately invited to give the Lenten sermons in the same church the following year, an invitation that would have been very flattering even to the most experienced of preachers.

The Priesthood

Devotion to the Eucharist and love of the Blessed Virgin were the heart and soul of Lawrence's spirituality. On the days when he was to receive Communion (daily Communion was not customary at this period), he used to remain in choir after the recitation of the nightly Divine Office to make a prolonged and fervent preparation. He was acutely conscious of the greatness of the eucharistic mystery, and as his ordination to the priesthood drew near, he experienced an increasingly severe struggle between his desire to offer the sacrifice of the Mass and his feeling of unworthiness. As had happened in the case of St. Francis himself, Lawrence's feeling of unworthiness grew and gained the upper hand, but happily a command from his superiors overcame his hesitation and on December 18, 1582, he was made a priest for all eternity. On December 26, the feast of St. Stephen, surrounded by his relatives and confreres, he celebrated his first solemn Mass in the church of the Most Holy Redeemer.

Chapter II

The Preacher

Preaching

IN THE course of his very varied career, Father Lawrence engaged in many different types of priestly activity for more or less extended periods of time. Yet preaching was his real life work, his special vocation, and the one at which he continued to labor from the first to the last day of his priestly ministry. We can say in truth that he never ceased to lavish from the pulpit the inexhaustible treasures of his learning. Hence we must examine with particular attention this facet of his life in order to see, even though briefly, its fundamental characteristics.

It was certainly a fortunate circumstance that Father Lawrence had been trained and formed as a preacher in a religious order which, from its very beginning, had resolutely rejected every departure from the simple mode of preaching the Gospel. As everyone knows, during the Renaissance formal Church preaching left much to be desired in content and manner. But the Capuchins' motto was always, "Return to the Gospel! Preach the Gospel!"

Our Saint appeared upon the scene and embarked on his apostolic activity at a propitious moment. During the first half of the sixteenth century, the Capuchins had aroused great interest and had won popular

19

acclaim by their preaching of the Gospel, and just when Lawrence was beginning his apostolate, the experiences of his predecessors were being reduced to practical formulae. We can be sure that he knew how to avail himself of his confreres' experience and to draw the greatest profit therefrom, profit not only for himself but also for others, for it appears that he wrote a short book on the practice of preaching entitled *Tractatus de modo concionandi*.

Not only was Father Lawrence endowed with all the physical, intellectual and moral gifts that go to make a great preacher, but he also knew, as few others did, how to develop these gifts and use them properly. He was robust in health, well-proportioned in body, handsome and dignified in appearance. Even as a youth his habitual cast of expression was one of natural gravity, and the passing years served only to render his features more mature and imposing. His forehead was high and his face, ruddy with health, was framed in a flowing auburn beard which fell to his chest, giving added majesty to his appearance. But it was his eyes especially that mirrored his inner power and the wide range of feeling of which he was capable. These eyes could shine with holy enthusiasm, or burn with indignation; they could sparkle with joy, be clouded with sadness or, as often happened, they could stream with tears.

His voice, too, was a faithful index of the emotions that surged within him, for it could express the most delicate feelings of his heart, and record the heavenly delights and rapture of divine love; but it could also roll like thunder and instill a holy fear in those who heard it. And his gestures, like his voice, could sometimes be so forceful and dramatic that they took his hearers' breath away.

Mind and Heart

These precious external gifts were vivified and, so to speak, activated by an irresistible force bursting forth from within. The Saint's whole life—spiritual and earthly—was marked by a fundamental theme, an intensity of feeling that seemed to know no bounds and that almost bordered on the pathological. It was providential that he also possessed a will strong enough and an intellect keen enough to counterbalance this intensity of emotion. Nevertheless we know that those who heard him preach received the impression that his feelings boiled within him like lava in a volcano which could erupt at any moment. Sometimes it even seemed that he would not be able to control himself and would be carried away by the violence and tumult of his emotions. It was at these times especially that the tears poured down his face and beard, soaking his habit and even falling to the ground.

Yet great as were his physical endowments and depth of feeling, his gifts of intellect were more outstanding still. His memory was so perfect, so unfailing, that he could rely upon it everywhere and at all times. Just as it had allowed him to retain every word of the Bible and to write down exactly a sermon he had heard while still a boy, so also it permitted him to preserve with great ease whatever could be useful to him in preaching. He once candidly confided to a confrere: "When I begin to preach, my mind and memory open out." As

21

he said this, he demonstrated with a movement of his hand, "how it was as if he saw in a book what he was preaching." [1] Because of this unusual gift, he was always prepared to preach and was able to speak extempore without the slightest difficulty.

As evidence of his ability to recall things rapidly and to think quickly, we have the testimony of his contemporaries and the fact that it is difficult to find corrections and repetitions in the original manuscripts of his writings. His small, swift, angular handwriting gives the impression of powerful thoughts pressing from within with irresistible force and finding welcome release as his pen travelled quickly over the paper. From his handwriting, too, one gets the impression of a truly exceptional clarity of thought and expression. In short, when we examine the Saint's writings, we find ourselves in the presence of a man with a quick mind overflowing with ideas and with the ability to express these thoughts clearly. And this is even more significant when we remember that he wrote in Latin.

Sermons and Writings

His devotion to preaching matched his facility of thought and expression. Advent, Lent, Sundays and the various feast days of the year saw him regularly in the pulpit and only the gravest and most pressing business could prevent him from preaching. Nevertheless, the care with which he prepared his sermons was more remarkable even than his assiduity in preaching them. No matter how often he had already spoken on a par-

[1] Deposition of P. Giovanni da Fossombrone, in *Proc. Ap. Gen.*, f. 16v.

22

ticular subject, he meditated upon it anew before each sermon and put down on paper the thoughts that occurred to him.

His preparation was unremitting, intense and prolonged. He used to retire to a secluded spot, to the chapel or his room, and there, with only the Bible and some sheets of paper, he would kneel down before a picture or statue of Our Lady, meditating upon the Gospel text that he was going to expound. Slowly his face would begin to glow, his chest would start to heave with the violence of his sighs and sobbing, his tears would flow and it was not unusual for fervent aspirations, half-suppressed moans and even cries of love to spring from his lips.

From time to time, as he knelt at this ardent meditation, which could last for several hours, he would take up his pen and commit to paper the thoughts which would form the basis of his sermon. Thus it was that, bit by bit, he accumulated the veritable mountain of manuscripts which were finally published not so long ago and which fill the eleven large volumes of his *Opera Omnia*. And certainly these eleven volumes do not contain all that he ever wrote, for a good number of his notes and sermons have been irrevocably lost.

Among his writings we find four series of sermons in Latin for each day of Lent, and the second of these series alone fills three volumes. In addition we also find the remains of two series of sermons in Italian for every day in Lent and the sermons for two other Lenten series of three weeks each. For Advent, he prepared at least six series of sermons as well as special sermons for the feasts of the Christmas season. In his *Dominicalia,* or sermons for each Sunday from Easter to Advent, there are two practically complete series and scattered here and there are traces of others. His sermons in honor of the apostles and other saints are collected in the *Sanctorale,* while his sermons on the Blessed Virgin are, for the most part, contained in his *Mariale,* about which we shall speak more later. In all, the matter he prepared for his sermons fills about 5,800 pages of his *Opera Omnia* and is a truly inexhaustible mine of material which, when reworked and properly applied, can be extremely useful even in our day. Again, all of us, especially those who must preach, can derive much benefit from the example which St. Lawrence left us by his unremitting preparation, his respect and love for the truth and the word of God. And this example is the more eloquent when we remember the weighty responsibilities and the important commitments which occupied his mind during his whole life.

Unfortunately the present biographical essay does not allow us to consider at length the various aspects of St. Lawrence's sermons and other writings. However, we can say that in the pages of his works we get a glimpse into the heart of a saint and can form some idea of the moral and religious preoccupations which engaged his mind. Even more; when we re-read his works attentively, we do not find it difficult to catch the echo of the battles he fought against the errors of his times. Here, too, we find the explanation of his frequent attacks on the state policy which the Venetian patricians applied most radically and unscrupulously and which was undoubtedly a menace to Catholic orthodoxy. His writings also explain his constant aversion to Aristotle's theories as they were explained and defended by certain philosophers with Averroistic tendencies, particularly at the

24

University of Padua. And we also find in his books the reason for the severity of his judgment on the prominent men of his day and on the nobility, whom he regarded as being ravaged by the fatal germs of intellectual and political inertia and by their dissolute morals. But we can deal more fully with all that later.

The Scriptures in His Preaching

In the meantime, however, even if we leave to one side all discussion of the other aspects of St. Lawrence's preaching, we cannot avoid drawing attention to a feature which was certainly the principal mark of his sermons, namely, the use he made of Holy Scripture.

In the first place, the Saint, faithful to the Capuchin tradition, always built and developed his sermons around the Gospel of the day or of the feast on which he was to preach. Furthermore, his exposition, his explanation of dogmatic and moral theology, and in fact his whole thought, were steeped in Holy Scripture, which became the connective tissue of all his discourses, the soul and life of his eloquence. Quotations from Scripture, either continuous passages or short texts, seem to fit naturally into his train of thought, and this feature, combined with his astounding knowledge of the holy books, shows a true identity between his mind and the message of the Bible. He thought like the Bible, his concepts were those of the Bible, he expressed himself in the language of the Bible and he drew from the Bible not only expressions, examples and citations but also an endless harvest of inspiration, comparisons and similes. No consideration or allusion, no matter how insignificant it was, failed to awaken in him a memory of the Scriptures. In his writings, every point is appropriately emphasized and underlined by a biblical reference, allusion or image. And his awe-inspiring knowledge of the Bible is revealed even better by his continued use of complete direct quotations and particularly by the uninterrupted stream of implicit references and veiled allusions, whether in the form of an adjective, a noun or the tone of a sentence. We feel that the sacred text was always present to him, creating and saturating the very atmosphere in which he lived, thought and acted. And all this lends to his words an extraordinary depth and a savor of unusual holiness.

Brilliant Success

The Saint's remarkable gifts of mind and body, coupled with his intense fervor and evident holiness, could not fail to work an irresistible charm on his hearers. Nature and grace combined to provide him with the best means of gaining an entrance to men's hearts, of arousing them and bringing them to God. Even during the first Lent that he preached at San Giovanni Nuovo in 1582 while he was still only a deacon, he won the admiration of the Venetians and moved them to tears. From then until the end of his life he continued to stir his listeners' hearts. An eye-witness reports: "He preached with so much love of God that he seemed to be afire and with so much hatred for sin that he stirred his listeners to the depths of their souls." [2]

In view of this, it is not surprising that the churches where he was to preach were literally besieged and that

[2] Deposition of Marc'Antonio Monti, in *Proc. Ap. Mil.,* p. 568.

the people used to arrive several hours early in order to secure a place. True, this happened especially during the last part of his life, yet there is no doubt that even at the start of his career he drew unusually large crowds.

His ability as a preacher, combined with his holiness, gave him immediate entry to the greatest pulpits of the day and made him one of the most renowned preachers in the Capuchin Order and even in the whole Church. It was not without good reason that, from his youth, he was often to be found preaching in the most important political and cultural centers such as Venice, where he preached several series of sermons, Padua, Verona, Vicenza, Rome, Ferrara, Genoa, Mantua, Naples, not to mention the work he did in Prague, the capital of the German Empire, and at Munich, where the Duke and Duchess of Bavaria often came to hear him.

Preaching to the Jews

Surely one of the most interesting aspects of Father Lawrence's apostolate was his activity among the Jews. This activity was not a mere sideline, as it were, with the Saint. He had it very much at heart, regarded it as being of great importance, and apparently engaged in it over a very long period of time. In fact, it was one of the three main branches of his apostolic activity, the other two being his preaching to the faithful and, later, to heretics.

This type of apostolate was in close harmony with the Church's policy after the Council of Trent. Reacting to the attacks of Protestantism, the Church was reorganizing not only to undertake a counterattack in the heartland of Europe but also to embark on the conver-

27

sion of the races recently discovered in the New World. But this widespread missionary activity did not lead the Church to neglect the home mission to the Jews.

Obviously, the Jews would never have come spontaneously to Christian preachers for instruction. Hence the necessity of having recourse to compulsion and of making attendance at sermons obligatory. The Church did not compel anyone to become a Catholic but she did oblige the Jews to attend instructions in the true Faith in the hope of aiding the work of their conversion.

Already from the thirteenth century obligatory sermons had formed part of the Church's legislation but they were stressed with special zeal in the second half of the sixteenth century. Popes Paul IV and St. Pius V had introduced them vigorously in Rome, and Gregory XIII gave them impetus and definite organization first in his Bull *Vices ejus* of September 1, 1577, and later in the Bull *Sancta Mater Ecclesia* of September 1, 1581.

The sermons were to be given each Saturday by a theologian or other learned and competent person and they were to be in Hebrew whenever possible. The subject was to be taken from the Old Testament, and every Jew twelve years old and over was obliged to attend them in his turn under pain of heavy fines. Although Gregory XIII died a few months after the promulgation of his second Bull on the subject and his successor, Sixtus V, practically abolished the obligatory sermons, Clement VIII later revived them officially.

Father Lawrence began his apostolate just at the time when preaching to the Jews was being reorganized and given its definitive form. Moreover, from the beginning of his priestly career, he had never failed to combine this difficult apostolate with his work of preaching to

28

St. Lawrence's Writing Implements. (*Capuchin Museum, Rome.*)

the faithful. During Lent, as well as on every other favorable occasion, he had always tried to gather around him the children of the Synagogue.

His longest and most important series of obligatory sermons was the one which he gave in Rome during the reign of Clement VIII, from 1592 until 1594. This series contributed more than any other to spreading his fame and to giving the pontifical authorities and the most eminent personages at the Vatican an appreciation of his worth. In view of the skill and ardor with which he preached, it was almost inevitable that his fame should be spread abroad. In accordance with Gregory XIII's request he used to preach in Hebrew at least for the greater part of each sermon. So well did he speak

29

ST. LAWRENCE BEING SENT BY CLEMENT VIII AS A MISSIONARY
TO AUSTRIA AND BOHEMIA. (*Painted by G. Guidi. Vatican Art
Gallery.*)

that the rabbis were amazed, particularly at his perfect pronunciation, and they even thought that he was a Jew turned Christian. The faithful, who were free to attend the sermons if they wished, were even more astonished at his knowledge of Hebrew than the Jews themselves. Thus we can readily see how news of the Capuchin's extraordinary skill soon spread in Rome and beyond.

"With Great Charity"

No less admirable than his skill was the kindness and patience which he showed toward his audience, who were often unruly and quarrelsome. We can gauge the Jews' reactions to the sermons from the fact that the ecclesiastical authorities had to adopt very energetic measures in order to restrain the unwilling listeners and keep even a semblance of order and silence.

Confronted as they were with restless and openly contemptuous audiences, the preachers did not always find it easy to remain calm and completely self-possessed. That they did preserve their composure shows that they must have had far more than ordinary virtue. It was not without reason that Gregory XIII had advised them to deal with their audiences "with great love and self-effacement." [3]

If there ever was a preacher who strove to follow the Pope's instructions in this matter, it was undoubtedly Lawrence. The charity he showed in his sermons amazed not only the religious and Catholic lay people who heard him but also the Jews themselves.

It is true that sometimes, when he saw the obstinacy of the Jews, he spoke very forcefully, yet he would im-

[3] The Bull *Sancta Mater Ecclesia.*

31

mediately soften the effect of his words by warm expressions of fraternal charity. One of his confreres relates that at times when Father Lawrence saw how unbending the Jews were, he would exclaim, "Obstinate people!" or use some other similar expression, yet right afterwards he would call them his brothers, wishing to convince them of the truth.[4] Another witness assures us that "when (Father Lawrence) preached to the Jews, he did not reproach them but rather called them his dear brothers and so softened their hearts that they were content to listen to him." Even more, at the end of his sermons, they used to approach him with gifts as a mark of esteem.[5]

Many interesting incidents occurred in connection with his preaching to the Jews, but we cannot pause to relate them here. Let us say merely that Father Lawrence's great kindness, combined with his outstanding ability, often succeeded in touching the hearts of the Jews and winning them to the truth and the Catholic Faith.

Lector

In addition to the three forms of the apostolate indicated above, Father Lawrence was engaged in another closely related activity, teaching his Capuchin brothers. Soon after his ordination to the priesthood, the superiors of the Province of Venice, who were well aware of

[4] Deposition of P. Ambrogio da Firenze, in *Proc. Ap. Ven.*, pars. i, f. 184v.
[5] Deposition of P. Andrea da Venezia, in *Proc. Ap. Ven.*, pars I, f. 159r.

his competence in philosophy and theology, conferred on him the office of Lector, a post which he seems to have held for about three years, from 1583 to 1586. Besides being responsible for the academic training of the clerics, the lector had to see to their spiritual formation as well. In other words, Father Lawrence, in addition to being his pupils' mentor in the sacred sciences, was also their spiritual director. And when we remember that in those days each group of students had only one lector who brought them through the whole course of studies from beginning to end, we can imagine the influence which each lector could exert on the hearts and souls of his pupils.

Unfortunately we do not possess any details on our Saint's lectorship. However, it seems that we must attribute to his influence certain moving examples of exceptional fervor among the young clerics at Venice. These young men thirsted so much for penance and mortification and were so eager to reach the heights of sanctity that their superiors had to restrain them. The Bonaventurian atmosphere which Father Lawrence created around him so attracted and influenced his pupils that sometimes their health was affected, some of them being consumed prematurely in the flames of their own fervor.

As regards the direction which the Saint's teaching took, we have good reason to believe that he kept to the same exegetical-dogmatic line which as a youth he himself had followed during his theological studies. This method, in addition to fanning the ardor of the pupils, also urged the lector on to an increasingly profound study of Sacred Scripture.

Scripture Studies

A fortunate chance has preserved for us in a Greek translation a short work which the Saint wrote during his lectorship when he was perhaps not yet twenty-five years old. The original was entitled *De numeris amorosis*,[6] and despite the author's comparative youthfulness, it attracted the attention of the learned men of the day and was considered worthy of being translated into other languages. It is true that it holds little appeal for modern tastes since it is an essay on the mystical and cabalistic meaning of the Hebrew name for God, a meaning which, when properly understood, shows men how God loves them and which urges them to love Him in return. Yet we must not forget that such literary works were the typical products of contemporary tendencies among Christians and Jews. At any rate, this book shows that from the first days of his priestly career, Father Lawrence's attention was turned toward Scripture for reasons other than the simple satisfaction of his personal devotion. He studied the Bible with the zeal of the scholar as well as with that of the saint, diligently searching out what was, or what seemed to him to be, the hidden inner meaning of the word of God.

Since this brief treatise of his came down to us by the merest chance, we cannot reasonably exclude the possibility that he may have written other and perhaps more imposing works of the same type that have since been lost. This theory is all the more tenable when we remember that a later work of his, *Explanatio in Ezechielem Prophetam,* has been lost despite its size and

[6] The full title is *De numeris amorosis mystice in divina Scriptura positis disquisitio,* in *Opera omnia,* vol. X-2, p. 417 ff.

importance. Happily we still have his *Expositio in Genesim,* which, however, is incomplete. Father Lawrence began it as part of the full commentary on the Bible about which he had dreamed from his youth. But although he never finished it, there is enough of it to demonstrate his singular aptitude for scriptural commentary.

The method he developed for studying the Bible compels our admiration. Unlike his approach in *De numeris amorosis,* his main concern in *Explanatio in Ezechielem Prophetam* is to find out and determine as accurately as possible the literal meaning of the text, for this seemed to him the only solid foundation upon which to base all other considerations. To achieve this aim he worked with extreme care and attention to detail.

First he quoted the text of the Latin Vulgate, then ordinarily the Hebrew text, next the Chaldaic paraphrase and, quite often, he then gave the Jerusalem Targum in his own Latin translation. In addition, he gave the Septuagint version as well as the versions of other ancient interpreters. Having thus established the exact reading of the text, he went on to expound the passage in question, at which task he was aided greatly by his extraordinary competence in Hebrew and his perfect knowledge of Christian and Jewish exegetes. The ease and assurance which he showed in choosing between the various interpretations and in proposing his own solution are both equally worthy of remark and admiration.

Naturally, much of the material in the *Explanatio* is now out of date. But no one could reasonably expect even such a man as St. Lawrence of Brindisi to be always and in every respect several centuries ahead of his time, particularly in the fields of philology, criticism, history and archaeology. Yet we can still admire his method, so surprisingly modern; his rare competence in biblical languages and, consequently, his serious philological preparation, and finally, the laudable balance he displays in evaluating the opinions of others and in stating his own solutions. Actually, his method can still serve as a model for exegetes, even for those who are able to devote their whole lives to the study of Scripture and who, unlike him, are not obliged to engage in a hundred and one other activities.

Chapter III

The Superior

Growing Fame

AFTER three years of teaching, Father Lawrence was elected guardian of Bassano del Grappa at the Provincial Chapter held at Verona in the spring of 1586. While the friary at Bassano del Grappa was not among the foremost houses of the Venetian Province, it had its own importance, for it was the novitiate house, and in accordance with the custom of the day, when Father Lawrence became guardian, he was also appointed master of novices. Hence his work of teaching young men was not interrupted but rather became even more delicate and significant. Yet his new offices did not prevent him from preaching as always. Besides speaking at Vicenza and other places, he preached the Lenten series of 1588 with great success in the cathedral of the beautiful little town of which he had become a resident.

With the Vicar General

In 1589, as closely as we can determine, he was assigned to preach the Lenten series in Cosenza in Calabria, but when he finished he did not return immediately to his province. Although we do not know the precise reasons for his remaining outside his province, it was evidently the result of arrangements made by the Superior General of the Order, who was just then on visitation to the provinces of southern Italy. In July of the same year we find Father Lawrence still in Naples, this time with the Superior General, Father Girolamo of Polizzi, who was presiding at the Provincial Chapter there.

These were not easy times for the Capuchin Superior General, because Cardinal Giulio Antonio Santori, Archbishop of Santa Severina and Protector of the Order, was interfering unduly in its internal affairs and in the government of the religious. Undeniably, the Cardinal had a special affection for the Capuchins, but he gave the impression that, in practice, the Order was under his complete jurisdiction and that he could freely exert his authority in its affairs. Thus his protection became a kind of oppression which was all the more galling because he did not hesitate to receive favorably certain discontented, scheming religious who had recourse to him against their superiors' decisions and enactments.

An instance of the Cardinal's undue interference on behalf of an insubordinate religious took place at the Provincial Chapter in Naples in 1589, and Father Girolamo of Polizzi was not slow in using drastic measures to correct the situation. After drawing up the charge against the religious, he sent Father Lawrence to Rome without delay to lay the matter before the Cardinal Protector and to persuade him to change his attitude. Father Lawrence succeeded in performing his mission quickly and in the most satisfactory manner, which won him his superior's gratitude, but which at the same time earned him the Cardinal's dislike.

Vicar Provincial of Tuscany

The Superior General showed his confidence in Father Lawrence in a practical way, for we believe that it was due to his indirect intervention that the Saint was elected Vicar Provincial of Tuscany that year. He did not want to accept the office, and his unwillingness is understandable, for he was still quite young, scarcely thirty years of age. The Cardinal Protector, not at all pleased with Lawrence's election, resolved to wait for an opportunity to intervene in the affairs of the province and rid himself of this young man who was far from being subservient to him. He did not have long to wait.

It seems that, after some months, certain dissatisfied religious came to him with complaints. Taking advantage of the General's absence on visitation in the other provinces, the Cardinal had a new Chapter convoked, hoping that Father Girolamo of Polizzi would not hear about it until too late and would have to accept its enactments as finished business.

But the General, who was then in the province of the Marches, did find out in time. Interrupting the visitation at once, he crossed the Apennines, although it was in the depths of winter, and descended on Florence just at the moment when the Chapter was about to begin. With the full force of his authority, he solemnly addressed the members of the Chapter and reconfirmed Father Lawrence of Brindisi in his new office. All of this happened in January, 1590.

Apparently the Saint encountered no more opposition. In the following year he was reconfirmed in office, as was the custom, and in 1592 he finished his three-year period as Vicar Provincial. Unfortunately, we have no record of his activity during these years. However, it does seem that during this period he was responsible for founding the friary at Lucignano in the Val di Chiana and the one at Arcidosso in the diocese of Chiusi.

In Rome

When his term of office as Vicar Provincial of Tuscany was over, Father Lawrence was called to Rome, where for two years he held the important position of preacher to the Jews. Certainly his name was already known in the capital of Christianity, but this new commission, which brought him into contract with many Cardinals and with the Supreme Pontiff himself, assured him of the highest esteem of the Roman authorities.

Father Girolamo of Polizzi also was able to profit by Father Lawrence's presence in Rome. As a sign of the high opinion he had of the Saint's knowledge, he entrusted to him the revision of the *Expositio in Regulam S. Francisci* which he himself had written and which he was then preparing for publication. Unfortunately, however, when the book was already in the press, the Church authorities forbade its publication. Father Girolamo had made the mistake of inserting in his *Expositio* three papal bulls defining and limiting the authority of the Cardinal Protector in the internal affairs of the Order, and Cardinal Santori had avenged

42

himself by having the book condemned. It was only after the Cardinal's death in 1606 that the book, slightly revised, was finally published.[1]

Vicar Provincial of Venice

At the Chapter held in Padua in the spring of 1594, Father Lawrence was elected Vicar Provincial of Venice. At first he was unwilling to accept, but in the end, despite his repugnance, he had to resign himself to undertaking the new office. At that period, the province of Venice was very extensive, stretching as it did from Gorizia to Lake Garda, and from Innsbruck to Mantua and Rovigo. In those days, the canonical visitation of the friaries had to be made twice each year and always on foot. We can imagine the sacrifices this demanded from a Provincial. Danger and accidents, even serious ones, were not unknown, but with the help of God (which was sometimes quite extraordinary), Father Lawrence succeeded in overcoming every difficulty without losing his serenity and joy of soul. Moreover, he imparted this serenity and joy to his travelling companions, and made the long journeys on foot from one friary to another seem shorter. For, whether he prayed or recited the Divine Office, engaged in edifying conversation or in learned discussions on scriptural problems or other subjects, he was so well able to hold his companions' attention that they almost forgot the tedium and weariness of their travels.

It was no rare occurrence for the Saints' confreres to see him enraptured and so absorbed in God that he

[1] Hieronymus a Politio, O.F.M.Cap., *Expositio in Regulam S. Francisci*, Naples, 1606.

43

seemed unconscious of everything that took place around him. His face would glow and his breast heave with uncontrollable ardor, while sighs of love and half-suppressed sobs escaped his lips. "O my Lord!" he would say, or more tenderly, "O my Queen!" and this tenderness was such that it astonished those who heard him.[2]

In the Tyrol

In 1593, in answer to the urgent entreaties of the Archduke Ferdinand and his wife Ann Catherine of Gonzaga, the Superior of the Order felt obliged to accept the foundation of a friary at Innsbruck. The building of the house was completed during Father Lawrence's term of office as Provincial, and in December, 1594, the new friary was dedicated at an unusually moving ceremony in which the Archduke and his wife along with the highest nobles of the region took part. But unfortunately, Father Lawrence was not able to be present at the dedication since it was midwinter and the Alps stood between him and Innsbruck.

Some time later, in 1596, Father Lawrence, at the request of Archbishop Wolfgang Theodoric von Raitenau, sent three religious to Salzburg to choose a site for a second friary in the Tyrol. However, grave complications soon developed. The Archbishop, who was both impetuous and imperious, was so deceived by malicious informants that he believed certain serious calumnies which he did not hesitate to hurl recklessly in the faces of the religious. He went even further and, disregarding the protests of the Capuchins, sought to

---

[2] Deposition of P. Ambrogio da Firenze, in *Proc. Ap. Ven.,* pars I, f. 181r.

S. LAURENTIUS A BRUNDUSIO

ST. LAWRENCE AT THE COURT OF MAXIMILIAN OF BAVARIA.
(Drawn by Pietro Labruzzi, engraved by Antonio Gregori.
Capuchin Museum, Rome.)

ST. LAWRENCE AT THE BATTLE OF ALBA REGALE AGAINST THE
TURKS. (*Painted by F. Grandi. Vatican Art Gallery.*)

build the friary to his own specifications, without regard for the rules laid down in the Constitutions of the Order. When Father Lawrence heard of these happenings he ordered the three friars to leave Salzburg immediately and return to Italy. Happily the Archbishop realized his mistake before it was too late, and the whole matter was settled to the satisfaction of both parties.

Definitor General

On May 31, 1596, the General Chapter met in Rome. From the events related so far, it is apparent that Father Lawrence's name was known to and highly esteemed by many of the members of the Chapter. Hence his election as second Definitor General came as no surprise.

Among the other decisions reached by this Chapter was the official introduction of the *Modus procedendi,* a short document setting down a method of judicial procedure and designed to guide the Major Superiors in the administration of punitive justice. This document, the first of its kind adopted by a religious order, is of particular interest to us because it is not improbable that Father Lawrence contributed to its formulation. In fact, if we are to believe one author, the Saint had previously written a short treatise entitled *Direttorio di diritto* from which the *Modus procedendi* itself was taken.

At this period, the Definitors General did not reside in Rome, so that when the Chapter ended, Father Lawrence returned to Venice, where in the spring of 1597 he finished his three years as Provincial. His natural ability, combined with his holiness and a more than human insight, made him a model provincial superior, so that he could truthfully be called "the consolation of all the friars." [3]

Guardian at Venice

After serving as Provincial, Father Lawrence had high hopes of being allowed to remain free of all cares of government, at least for a short period. But he soon had to accept the fact that all his prospects of rest had vanished for a long time because, despite the existing laws regarding tenure of office, the superiors wanted him as Guardian of the friary of the Most Holy Redeemer, the most important house in the province. However, in order to have more opportunity to practice obedience in some fashion, he voluntarily submitted to the orders and wishes of the friar who had been assigned to take care of his needs. At a nod from this friar, he would stop praying or studying or leave whatever else he was doing.

At Ferrara

It seems that Father Lawrence was Guardian at Venice for only one year because in 1598, after he had preached the Lenten series in Vicenza, we find him in Ferrara. At the beginning of that year Ferrara had passed from under the dominion of the Este family to the Holy See, and on May 8th Pope Clement VIII came in person to take ceremonial possession of the city.

[3] Deposition of P. Ambrogio da Firenze, in *Proc. Ap. Ven.,* pars I, f. 180r.

Among the problems raised by the change in government was the question of the Jews, who had been in high favor and had enjoyed great freedom under the rule of the Estes. For one thing, they had not been compelled to attend the obligatory sermons, and it appears that the Roman authorities, wishing to solve this problem, sent Father Lawrence to Ferrara as the best man for the task.

Vicar Provincial of Switzerland

While he was working with his usual zeal at the charge entrusted to him, the Saint was dismayed to hear that the Swiss Capuchins had overwhelmingly elected him their Vicar Provincial at their Chapter in late September, 1598. It is possible that this surprising development was due to the suggestion of Father Girolamo of Sorbo, the Vicar General, who had just finished his visitation of the Swiss province. However, Father Lawrence never went to Switzerland, and the province was ruled instead by a substitute or pro-Vicar Provincial. Yet this did not prevent the Saint from attending the General Chapter of 1599 as the Superior of the Swiss province.

Chapter IV

The Warrior

Urgent Summons to Germany

O N MAY 28, 1599, at the twenty-third General Chapter of the Order, the Saint's colleagues reaffirmed their confidence in him by electing him Definitor General once more. The most pressing problem confronting this Chapter was the organization of a missionary expedition to Prague, the heart of the German Empire. At the close of the sixteenth century, the Capuchins were, with the Jesuits, incontestably the most fervent and most renowned missionaries in the whole of Europe. Although it was not until 1574 that the Holy See had granted them permission to establish themselves in the countries beyond the Alps, they had increased rapidly there and had engaged in intense missionary activity in France, the Netherlands, Lorraine, and Savoy, where they had given St. Francis de Sales considerable help in evangelizing the people of the Chablais district and had penetrated as far as Geneva, the stronghold of Calvinism. At the invitation of St. Charles Borromeo, they had labored in the Valtellina valley to rekindle the courage of the Catholics suffering under the oppression of the heretics. Despite all opposition, they had gone into the Catholic cantons of Switzerland and had established themselves so firmly

53

there that they merited to be reckoned among the pillars of the Church in that region. Likewise in the Tyrol, at Salzburg and Innsbruck, as we have already seen, they had planted firm roots, as they had done also in Venezia Giulia, across from Carnia and Carinthia, which Protestantism threatened to engulf.

This generous and fearless missionary work against heresy had won general esteem and recognition for the Capuchins and had earned them a position in the foremost ranks of the Catholic counterattack at points where Protestantism was already a very serious threat. It was just this great renown that led several important personages in the German Empire to make insistent demands for their intervention and assistance in stemming the rising tide of heresy. Thus it was that in 1597, after several unfortunate attempts upon which we need not dwell here, the Archbishop of Prague, Zbynek Berka von Duba, informed the Vicar General of the lamentable state of religion in his diocese and begged him to send him some Capuchins. To assure himself of a speedy and favorable reply, the Archbishop enlisted the support of several cardinals and of other influential people at the Roman court. As before in the case of similar requests, the Capuchins were hesitant in acceding, since they were afraid that they would not be able to observe fully the Rule and Capuchin Constitutions in the new territory, which was so different in customs and in climate. But the decision of Clement VIII put an end to all their problems and difficulties. During the General Chapter of 1599, the Pope, through the medium of the Cardinal Protector, commanded the Capuchins to accept the mission in Prague without more ado.

Commissary General of Germany

When the Pope commanded, the friars had no
choice but to obey. After discussing the best method
of executing the papal order, they decided to send to
Germany a team of missionaries, twelve in number
like the apostles, under the leadership of Father Lawrence. They could not have chosen a better man. A
vigorous forty years of age, unusually experienced in
governing, fairly well acquainted with the customs and
the political and religious condition of the countries
beyond the Alps, a warrior and solid theologian, ani-
mated by love of God and burning zeal, Father Lawrence seemed to be just the man for the mission. Perhaps the only thing he lacked was sufficient knowledge
of the language to allow him to use it in the sacred ministry. However, he did know it well enough for everyday
purposes.

His companions, too, were exceptionally fervent and
zealous religious, men of more than ordinary holiness
and culture. Some of them had even snatched eagerly
at the chance of going to Germany in the hope of suffering martyrdom at the hands of the heretics there.
With such subjects as these, Father Lawrence had nothing to do but restrain their enthusiasm and desire for
the martyr's crown.

The twelve missionaries were ordered to join forces
in Venice, from whence, at the end of July, they set out,
passing through Verona, Trent, Innsbruck and Vienna.
During their journey, they had a foretaste of what
awaited them in the mission ahead. Beyond Innsbruck
and particularly in upper Austria, the people, who were

55

mostly heretics, did not spare them insults, mockery and even blows, yet it would have taken much more than that to intimidate and discourage men who were seeking martyrdom. But despite the urgency with which they had travelled, they were forced to mark time when they finally arrived in Vienna on August 28.

In Prague

Just at this period, Bohemia and Moravia were being ravaged by the plague, so that it would have been rash and useless for the missionaries to have undertaken the voyage to Prague immediately. Fearing infection, the Papal Nuncio and the imperial court had already left that city, and the people of the region, who were almost all heretics, would have fled from the Capuchins as if from mad dogs. Moreover, as a result of their gruelling journey under the blazing August sun, several of the religious were exhausted and in poor health. In the end, Father Lawrence himself, despite his driving zeal, also fell ill, as did almost all of the missionaries.

The possibility that the friars had caught the plague frightened away many people who would otherwise have helped them, with the result that the religious were reduced to a state of isolation and abandonment that would have taken the heart out of anyone less heroic. But, with God's help, this trial also passed. And when, with the lessening of the summer heat, the violence of the plague began to decrease, Father Lawrence decided to resume his journey with those of his companions who felt strong enough to travel. The Archduke Matthias, who ruled Austria in the name of his brother the Emperor, invited the rest of the missionaries to remain in Vienna with the idea of founding a friary there.

The Saint and his companions left Vienna in the beginning of November, arriving a few days later in Prague, where the citizens received them with abuse and insults. However, the Archbishop's cordial welcome did much to offset the hostile attitude of the heretics, for the good prelate extended to the missionaries the hospitality of his palace for more than a week. Then, until a friary could be built, he gave them charge of a church beside the archdiocesan hospital, on the right bank of the Moldau river, near the Charles Bridge, which was famous both for its beauty and for its connection with the martyrdom of St. John Nepomucene.

Religious and Political Conditions in Bohemia

As we have already indicated, a large part of the population of the city of Prague and of Bohemia as a whole were heretics. Only two faiths were officially recognized, Catholicism and Hussitism, but the adherents of other sects took refuge under the name Hussite, and in reality every one of the heresies hatched in Germany in the preceding years had partisans here.

If the Catholic priests of the region had been a compact group full of zeal, the religious situation, although grave, would not have seemed desperate. But unfortunately, with the exception of the Jesuits, almost all the regular and secular clergy were in a sorry state both intellectually and morally. Only too many of the clergy were completely uninterested in ministering to souls, and not a few of them were leading scandalous and depraved lives.

57

While religious conditions were bad, the political atmosphere was certainly no better. Although Catholics were in the minority, they still retained a majority of the administrative offices in the kingdom of Bohemia and in the empire generally. Yet this advantage was for the most part rendered useless by the Emperor's character. His eternal indecision, his repugance to applying himself to the affairs of government, and the isolation in which he wrapped himself, made difficult and almost impossible any timely intervention in the numerous serious problems that agitated the political and religious life of the kingdom and the empire. It seemed that the Emperor, Rudolph II, had time only for his favorites, the astronomers and the astrologists, the alchemists and the artists. Even worse than that, at the time the Capuchins arrived in Prague, his physical and mental condition was deteriorating rapidly, and he was often beset by fixed ideas and frequently lapsed into insanity. In short, everything contributed to an appalling paralysis of the functions of the government at a time when a strong hand and a firm policy were needed as never before.

Apostolic Fervor

Having settled themselves as well as possible near the archdiocesan hospital, Father Lawrence and his companions began to officiate daily and preach three times a week in the church confided to their care. The Catholics of Prague, happy at the arrival of the Capuchins, began to flock to the church beside the hospital. Not only did the average devout citizens come but also important people such as the High Chancellor of the kingdom of Bohemia. Even the heretics themselves were not long able to resist the attraction of the missionaries and soon they, too, attended Father Lawrence's sermons. However, their presence in his audience did not cause the Saint to turn a blind eye to their errors. Instead, he attacked and refuted their false teachings courageously and implacably. His knowledge of the Scriptures was particularly useful to him here since it allowed him to supply abundant documentary proof of Catholic doctrine and to show the inconsistency of the heretics' claims.

Not content with the work being done in the church, the Saint found a way to approach an ever greater number of people. With his consent, one or another member of the aristocracy would gather together a group of friends and acquaintances to discuss religious problems. Father Lawrence would then appear at these meetings, bringing to bear upon the questions discussed the whole weight of his knowledge of theology and Scripture. In this way, his patient, unremitting teaching removed so many barriers and prejudices that great sympathy with the friars' aims was generated and the prospect of a fruitful apostolate became daily more promising.

The Other Side of the Coin

Despite all this, the heretics who approached the Capuchins or who did not rebuff them were only a minority. The missionaries' activity and intrepidity in combating heresy only enraged most of their adversaries, who lost no opportunity to avenge themselves. During the friars' first months in Prague, the heretics' boldness and effrontery were increased by the fact that the Emperor and almost all the authorities had left the city for fear of the plague, which had not yet fully subsided, and had gone to Pilsen.

When the missionaries went out to seek alms or to minister to souls, they were taking their lives in their hands. If they were lucky, they were merely insulted and mocked, but more than once they returned home bruised and bleeding. Father Lawrence suffered with the rest of the friars, and his secretary assures us that "several times the heretics beat him and knocked him down." [1]

While things were like this in Prague, they were no better in Vienna. Here the Capuchins had even been fired on, and it was only by pure chance that none of them was killed. If one adds to all this the suffering they endured from the cold, unusually intense that year, one will get a rough idea of the trials the missionaries had to bear that winter.

The First Three Friaries

With the approach of good weather, plans were made for the erection of the friary at Prague. Despite many great difficulties, Father Lawrence succeeded in getting a site on the left bank of the Moldau, in the best section of the city, not far from the famous cathedral of St. Vitus and close to the imperial gardens. On May 23, in the presence of an unusually large gathering of Catholics and Protestants, the cross was raised and the first stone laid.

Immediately afterwards, the Saint set out for Vienna, where, during the winter, the Capuchins had also

[1] Deposition of P. Ambrogio da Firenze in *Proc. Ap. Ven.,* pars I, f. 187v.

CRUCIFIX CARRIED BY ST. LAWRENCE DURING HIS TERM OF OFFICE AS VICAR GENERAL. (*General Curia, O.F.M.Cap., Rome.*)

ST. LAWRENCE. (*Artist unknown.*)

worked zealously and had earned the esteem and veneration of the city's Catholics. When he arrived there, he found that only a last few obstacles had to be overcome before the preparations could be made for the erection of the cross and the laying of the first stone of the new friary. The ceremony itself was made more solemn still by the presence of the Bishop of Nitra, Franz Forgatz, and of the Archduke and his court.

Having finished his business in Vienna, Father Lawrence hastened on his way to Graz, the capital of Styria, where the future Emperor, the twenty-one-year-old Archduke Ferdinand, held court. In the heat of the battle against the Protestants and with the firm resolve to bring about an effective Catholic reform, Ferdinand also had implored the Capuchins to help him. And now, by order of the Pope, Father Lawrence had come to prepare for a new foundation in Graz.

The young Archduke's full cooperation speeded the approach of the opening ceremony, and on August 10, the Apostolic Nuncio, Monsignor Girolamo Porcia, personally laid the first stone with great solemnity in the presence of the Archduke and his mother and of a great gathering of nobles and commoners.

After the ceremony, Father Lawrence lost no time in returning to Vienna.

Difficulties and Uncertainty

He had scarcely reached the city when he was met by a confrere who urged him to go immediately to Prague. On June 10, Rudolph II had finally decided to leave Pilsen and return to his capital, Prague. As he passed near the place where the Capuchins were going to build their friary, he had shown his satisfaction with the friars' arrival as well as with their choice of site. However, the ruler's feelings toward the religious were to change drastically in a short time.

We have already mentioned Rudolph's mental instability and growing insanity. During the latter part of 1600, his fixed ideas and lapses into madness became more frequent and more serious. Encouraged by some of his heretical friends, he had become convinced that the Holy See was working through its nuncios and emissaries to strip him of his authority and deny him any power. Hence he began to nurture a growing defiance and hostility to anyone in good standing with Rome and her representatives. This included the Capuchins, who eventually became the target for Rudolph's special acrimony.

The heretics, hoping that the time had finally come for settling their accounts with their adversaries, set about planting in the ruler's sick mind the suspicion that the Capuchins were nothing but spies for the Pope and that they had come to Prague with the idea of assassinating him as a Dominican had done to Henry III of France some years before. Furthermore, a famous Protestant astronomer who enjoyed the Emperor's full confidence used all his skill and wiles to convince him of the truth of these allegations.

Rudolph II, overwhelmed by fear and obsessions, was reduced to such a pitiable state that he went in fear of his life. Making up his mind to rid himself of the friars, he repeatedly sent requests to the archbishop to have them expelled at once. But that was precisely what the prelate was not inclined to do. In fact, when the Emperor became more insistent, the archbishop replied that he would rather leave himself than expel the Capuchins.

Next, the Emperor tried to force his ministers to get rid of the friars, but they respectfully replied that, since they hadn't invited the religious to come, they were in no position to make them leave. Finally, Rudolph turned to the Nuncio, ordering him to remove the Capuchins, whose presence had become a nightmare and a torment to him. But the Nuncio, with great diplomacy, was also able to avoid carrying out the Emperor's command.

And what of the Capuchins while all this backstage maneuvering was going on? Under Father Lawrence's leadership, they fought their own battle calmly and firmly. Upon his return from Vienna, the Saint had immediately realized the gravity of the situation and had exhorted his companions to "fight the good fight" against "the devil unchained." They intensified their prayers, disciplines and penances, while he, in addition, made more urgent appeals to the imperial and ecclesiastical authorities.

But despite all these efforts, a point was reached where even the Catholic ministers of state were forced to conclude that the Capuchins would have to go. Father Lawrence's unwillingness to leave was not due to obstinacy; he merely wanted to have the expulsion order put into writing because he did not wish to take upon himself the grave responsibility of ordering the friars to depart from Prague.

However, no matter how long he waited, the order did not come, although it was known that the decree of expulsion had lain open on the Emperor's desk for several days waiting for the signature needed to render it effective. Finally, early in 1601, because of various providential circumstances and as a result of Father Lawrence's efforts, the friars received, not an order to leave, but assurance that the Emperor was beginning to regain his calm and that the danger of expulsion was growing less. Now more loved and respected than ever, the Capuchins were able to continue their good work and finish building their friary.

Alba Regale

An incident which occurred in October, 1601, had much to do with spreading and increasing in Germany and elsewhere Father Lawrence's renown as a saint. Toward the middle of that year, two officers of the imperial army each asked for two Capuchins to minister to the spiritual needs of the troops they were about to lead into Hungary against the Turks. Ten years before, after fifteen years of uneasy peace, the hostilities between the Turks and the imperial forces had broken out again. The struggle had dragged on without any brilliant strategies or decisive victories, with the fortunes of war first going to one side and then to the other, while the already ravaged Hungarian plain was devastated still more.

Father Lawrence tried to answer with a polite refusal the request for four military chaplains, for he had only a few religious at his disposal and he well knew the physical and spiritual dangers of army camps. Yet when he found that he could not evade the request, he decided to go himself as one of the chaplains. Leaving Vienna with the Archduke Matthias, the Commandant General of the army, he arrived on October 9 at the encampment near Alba Regalis (then Stuhlweissenburg, now Szekesfehervar) in the middle of Hungary. This strong point had been regained about a month earlier by the imperial forces, and now the main problem was to hold it against the enemy, who were massing their forces nearby. In order to maintain greater maneuverability, the Christian army stationed a large garrison at the central point and then drew back some distance to the hills, where they took up a strongly defended position. It was here that, on October 9, Father Lawrence arrived in the company of the Archduke Matthias, just in time to hear the sound of the arquebuses and cannon.

The situation was not encouraging. As against the seventeen or eighteen thousand soldiers of the imperial army, the Turks were able to send into the field more than sixty thousand men, well armed and well equipped. Under such conditions, prudence bade the Christians to remain entrenched in their fortified positions and to refuse the enemy's challenge to fight on the open plain.

While waiting for the Turks to attack, the Archduke took the opportunity to stiffen the morale of his disheartened troops by asking Father Lawrence to address them. Nothing could have pleased the Saint more. Taking his inspiration from Sacred Scripture, he spoke with all the fervor and vehemence at his command. He recalled the lofty aims for which they were fighting and offered to lead them into battle with the crucifix in his hand. These were not just empty words, for during the days that followed, when the enemy attacked, Father Lawrence was in the thick of the battle. Exposed to salvos of artillery, to rifle fire and to flights of arrows, he did not flinch or retreat, but rode so far to the front of the army and seemed so reckless that the officers were forced to remonstrate politely with him. Several times he was nearly killed but somehow he always managed to escape unharmed. All types of projectiles—arrows, bullets and cannon balls—seemed to lose their momentum and fall to the ground when they came near him. Eyewitnesses have left us descriptions of happenings that appeared impossible and that really cannot be explained in human terms. Even the keen blades of the Turkish scimitars could not harm him, for he seemed to be protected on all sides by an invisible shield, with the result that the Turks took him for a sorcerer and magician, while the Christian soldiers tried to stay as near as possible to him in battle, believing they were safest there. His soldier companions used to kiss the wonder-working crucifix which he proffered to them and ask for his blessing. To the Christian forces, his presence as he went tirelessly from troop to troop was the best guarantee of ultimate victory, while his words of exhortation and encouragement raised their spirits and redoubled their strength.

So it came about that, despite the smallness of their army, despite the vacillation and mistakes of their leaders, and despite the panic that occasionally gripped some of the troops, the Christian forces prevailed. The Turks, worn out, discouraged, and rebellious after suffering several resounding defeats, withdrew from the battlefield. For that year at least, Alba Regalis was saved.

Loreto

Returning to Prague after the epic events in Hungary, Father Lawrence prepared to go to Rome where the General Chapter was to be convened in May of the following year. The Catholics of Prague, loath to lose him just when his prestige would best serve their cause, tried to get him to stay by appealing to the Apostolic Nuncio, but they had to resign themselves to letting him go.

Having made final arrangements for the continuance of the mission, the Saint left in the depths of winter and despite the ice, snow and hardships that lay in wait for him on the long journey. His haste in departure was due to his desire to arrive as soon as possible at Loreto, where he had resolved to spend the whole of Lent. Entering Italy through the Tyrol and the valley of the Adige, he stopped briefly at Mantua where, in the name of the Emperor, he carried out a diplomatic mission to Duke Vincenzo Gonzaga. Then after a brief visit to Venice to greet his confreres and relatives, he went down along the Adriatic coast to Loreto. Here, at the celebrated shrine of Our Lady, he passed the Lent of 1602, spending hours and even entire days in communion with God and the Blessed Virgin, in serving Mass, and in speaking with the pilgrims, increasing their love for the Mother of God. This was his way of gaining spiritual refreshment and recuperating from the fatigue of his missionary work in preparation for new and still more arduous tasks.

Chapter V

The Vicar General

Vicar General

O N MAY 24, 1602, the members of the General Chapter almost unanimously elected Father Lawrence Vicar General of the order. At the same time, however, they confided to him the task of visiting all the provinces beyond the Alps, a commission that was far from being easy, especially because he would not avail himself of any dispensation even during the longest and most exhausting journeys. Only one other Vicar General, Father Girolamo of Sorbo, had succeeded in making this visitation, at a time when the Order was not yet so widespread, and then only by travelling on horseback, for which a dispensation was required.

When the Chapter ended, the new Vicar General left immediately for Assisi to beg the blessing of St. Francis. From here he went up through the Marches to Loreto to ask Our Lady's blessing also. Then he embarked on the northern route, through Ravenna, along the course of the River Po and across Lombardy. Toward the middle of July, he made the visitation of the Swiss Province, and on August 2, he held the Provincial Chapter at Baden.

From Baden he travelled quickly westwards and on August 9 reached Salins in the Franche Comté, where

73

he was received with many marks of love and devotion. The affection with which he was greeted increased as he passed through Dôle and Lorraine and reached its peak in the low countries where the people spread grass and flowers along his path and came out to meet him in procession singing the *Te Deum*.

At Liége a severe attack of lumbago compelled him to rest for a while. Already at Senigallia in the Marches this ailment had forced him to discontinue briefly his journey northwards, but this time his suffering was so great that he almost died. Yet as soon as he was on his feet once more he took to the road again, wearing only his habit next his skin, as was his custom, and disregarding pain, weariness, and cold.

After holding the Chapter at Arras on October 10, 1602, he made the visitation of the very extensive province of Paris and went on to visit the province of Bourgogne, which included Savoy. On January 4, 1603, he held the Chapter at Lyons, after which he turned south to visit first Provence and then Aquitaine, where, on April 11, he convoked the Chapter at Toulouse. Finally, he began the visitation of the immense Iberian Province which was composed of Rousillon, Catalonia, Aragon, and the kingdom of Valencia. At the conclusion of this gigantic tour he presided at the Chapter on June 20 in Barcelona. Thus in less than a year he had completed the onerous task which the General Chapter had confided to him.

The Italian Provinces

Father Lawrence did not intend to rest from his labors, but took advantage of the first convoy of ships leaving the port of Barcelona to sail to Italy where he wished to make the visitation of the numerous provinces of the peninsula. Toward the middle of July he was in Genoa, ready to set out once more on foot to visit the friars there, but because of a combination of circumstances, the Chapter had already been held some weeks before in that province, which included Piedmont. Hence the Saint did not think it opportune to make the visitation there, and he continued his journey by boat at the leisurely pace of the day.

In September he was in Sicily, where he visited the provinces of Palermo, Syracuse and Messina before going on to those of Reggio Calabria, Catanzaro and Cosenza. At the end of March he reached the province of Otranto, where he was able to revisit his beloved town of Brindisi, whose inhabitants gave him the warmest and most joyful of welcomes. Here on the feast of the Annunciation in 1604 he preached to his fellow citizens from the same pulpit from which he had spoken as a child.

Going north along the peninsula, he visited the provinces of Bari and Salerno where, toward the middle of June, 1604, he received the joyful news that Father Anselmo of Monopoli had been made a cardinal. Father Anselmo was the first Capuchin to receive the purple, and the General, when announcing the honor to the Order, recommended that all the friars celebrate it in a fitting manner. After this, when he had finished the visitation of the provinces of Naples and Foggia, he went on up to Abruzzi, the Marches and Umbria, and by the beginning of 1605 he had completed the visitation of Tuscany. He probably intended to visit northern Italy as well, but as at Senigallia and Liége, pain and ill

75

health made him change his plans and forced him to slow down. At all events, after holding the Provincial Chapter at Florence, he was unable to travel northwards because he had already promised to preach the Lenten series in the church of Spirito Santo in Naples. Hence he returned south to sunny Campania and, to make up for the Lents when he had been unable to preach, he added to the usual morning sermon another one in the evening on the Hail Mary and devotion to Our Lady. His three-year term of office was coming to a close but he still had work to do, for there was one province in central Italy which he had not visited, the Roman Province. Accordingly he made this visitation and held the Chapter at Frascati on May 4, 1605.

"The Holy General"

Considering the events we have just related, we do not think it an exaggeration to describe as gigantic the trek which the Saint had made across the face of Europe. He travelled everywhere on foot, in winter and in summer, in pouring rain or blistering heat, crossing rivers and marshes, mountains and plains, through ice and snow, without allowing himself a moment's rest, sometimes walking twenty-five, thirty, or even forty miles a day. One thing alone was able to stop him—illness or pain so severe that it chained him to his bed and brought him to the brink of death. But even then, he had no sooner gained his feet than he once more set out undaunted. He had no use for medicines and only with difficulty could he be persuaded to take them.

Even during the most arduous journeys, he continued to observe minutely the austere customs, prolonged fasts and rigorous abstinence of the order. Naturally, his body suffered from the penances he imposed on it, so that he sometimes arrived at the friaries in a pitiable state of exhaustion. Yet even then he would not accept dispensations or special treatment. At mealtime he partook only of the common food and at night he slept on a straw pallet like the other religious. The example of his austere life won him the admiration of all, including his travelling companions. His warm friendliness to everyone, even to the humblest of the religious, and his humility, like that of another St. Bonaventure, inspiring him to wash the dishes in the friary kitchen, were further sources of wonder and edification to those who witnessed them.

His example certainly urged on the friars toward a more perfect life and more exact observance of the Rule and Constitutions. But he was not content with giving example, for he was convinced that his office as Vicar General demanded that he should be, in every province, the guardian of the spirit of St. Francis. We can judge how dear that spirit was to him by the ordinances which he laid down in various provinces and which were a continual, insistent, and energetic recall to the traditional austerity of the Order and particularly to the strictest poverty. When it was a question of preserving the spirit of the Order, he did not recoil from employing stern measures and severe punishment. When he found transgressions he acted decisively even in the case of distinguished religious or provincial superiors. However, ordinarily he preferred to treat everyone with fatherly kindness. In order to urge the religious on to perfection, he used to exhort them in words that moved them to tears. One witness relates that "as he spoke, his heart seemed to leap from his breast." All of this, along with the wonders that occurred on his travels, amply justified the name given him by the religious and by the faithful, "the holy General."

Chapter VI

The Hammer of Heretics

O N MAY 27, 1605, the General Chapter was held at Rome and Father Lawrence was finally freed from his burdensome office. After returning to his own province of Venice, he again went to Loreto to thank Our Lady for her protection during the three arduous years of his term as Vicar General. He was now free of all the cares of superiorship, but rest was not for him. He had known that the people of Prague had sadly regretted his leaving the city and, at the beginning of his term as General, he had tried to make up for his departure by sending Father Mattia of Salò, a holy friar and noted preacher. But Father Mattia, who was now over sixty-six years of age, had just been recalled to Italy by the new General, Father Silvestro of Assisi, and the citizens of Prague felt the loss of Father Lawrence more than ever.

Furthermore, the war against the Turks in Hungary was still being waged with doubtful results. Father Lawrence's deeds during the campaign of 1601 were still vividly remembered and everyone, particularly the soldiers, wanted to have him back. Therefore, the Emperor, no doubt at the suggestion of one of his Catholic ministers, instructed his ambassador to the Holy See to ask the new Pope, Paul V, to send the Capuchin once more across the Alps. Meanwhile, Father Lawrence had gone to preach the Lenten sermons of 1606 at Aversa in Campania. In the spring of that year, he received the order there to go to Germany. He first returned to his province, but was soon on his way to his new assignment with several companions.

Donauwörth

Travelling swiftly across the Tyrol and Bavaria, he arrived in a short while at Donauwörth on the right bank of the Danube on the southern border of the High Palatinate. The people of Donauwörth were almost all heretics so that as the Saint and his companions went through the streets they were subjected to hostile demonstrations, sarcasm, and insults.

The few remaining Catholics had taken refuge around the Benedictine Abbey of the Holy Cross in a remote suburb, and it was here that the Capuchins went seeking shelter. The monks described to Father Lawrence the sad conditions under which they had to live, for the heretics never ceased to harass them. The latest sacrilegious incident had occurred only a few weeks before, on the feast day of St. Mark. On that day, in accordance with Catholic custom and in virtue of their right to freedom of worship, the monks had been walking in procession through the streets of the town when they were attacked and driven off with blows while their crucifix was broken and their banners torn to shreds. The monks, through their ecclesiastical superior, the Bishop of Augsburg, had appealed to the imperial authorities in Prague, but no one knew when these authorities would finally intervene.

ST. LAWRENCE OVERWHELMING A HERETIC. (*An engraving in the Capuchin Museum, Rome.*)

LETTER OF ST. LAWRENCE TO HIS FRIEND, P. REMIGIO DA BOZ-
ZOLO. (*Capuchin Archives, Bolzano.*)

Father Lawrence had just had a practical demonstration of the way in which the inhabitants of Donauwörth practised freedom of religion and so, aflame with zeal for the rights of Catholics, he promised to bring the state of affairs to the attention of the Nuncio and the imperial court. Upon reaching Prague, he was received with great joy by the Catholics of the city and, with characteristic energy, he immediately set about laying the matter of Donauwörth before influential people. Furthermore, he did not hesitate when preaching to give broad hints and to make unmistakable allusions to those who were remiss in taking appropriate action. But it did not take him long to see that his allusions and hints were having no effect. Hence he decided to have done with diplomacy and to denounce frankly and with pitiless clarity the weak-kneed policy of the government that was allowing everything to go to rack and ruin.

His denunciation created immediate excitement because the Nuncio, all the Catholic ambassadors, and many important people from the court and the city used to come regularly to hear him preach. But the guilty parties were so enraged by his reprimands that he deemed it wise to accept the invitation of Maximilian of Bavaria to go to Munich until calm had been restored in Prague.

Duke Maximilian had probably met Father Lawrence when the Saint passed through Munich on his way to Prague but he had undoubtedly known him by renown even before that. Now he was counting greatly on the Capuchin's sanctity to obtain from God a favor very close to his heart. His wife, Elizabeth of Lorraine, had for a long time shown such marked signs of mental and spiritual disturbance that everyone thought that she

85

was possessed. The Duke, therefore, had invited Father Lawrence precisely for the purpose of performing an exorcism on her. In seeking to cure the Duchess, the Saint himself prayed much and got other people to do likewise; he fasted and did penance. Time and time again he had to repeat the exorcism in the private chapel of the court, but finally God granted the desired favor and the Duchess was cured.

During Father Lawrence's stay in Munich, he and the Duke were able to get to know each other very well, and they conceived such a profound esteem for each other that they formed a friendship that was destined to endure and increase until the end of their days. It was then also that Father Lawrence became the Duke's confidant, privy counsellor, and spiritual director. During their conversations they undoubtedly spoke of the serious problem of Donauwörth and perhaps they also drew up together a common plan of action. At any rate, upon his return to Prague, the Saint, by means of private consultations and pointed sermons, was able to set in motion the rusted cogs of the imperial machinery of government while, in the meantime, the Duke of Bavaria and others kept insisting that a decision be reached. The citizens of Donauwörth were asked several times to keep the peace, but they remained so rebellious that the imperial ban was proclaimed against them. Duke Maximilian was ordered to put the ban into effect and he acted promptly and decisively by going at once to Donauwörth where he restored full liberty of worship to the Catholics.

Everyone, the Emperor, the Nuncio, and the ministers, were satisfied with the outcome of the affair, but Father Lawrence was perhaps the happiest of all. Later he was able to report objectively and without sham modesty that "it was well known that if Brother Lawrence of Brindisi had not been in Prague . . . nothing would have been done." [1]

Fight Against Heresy

While the serious situation at Donauwörth was being discussed at the imperial court, other events in Prague caught Father Lawrence's attention and spurred him to intervene energetically. The Protestants were taking advantage of the continued vacillation and inactivity of Rudolph II and his ministers to advance their cause more each day. The Saint's close acquaintance with the most important people of the day allowed him to keep well-informed about what was going on behind the scenes, and he let nothing pass without comment. Vigorously he denounced from the pulpit every concession to, and compromise with, the heretics, and as time went on, his preaching became more inexorable and effective.

One episode will suffice to show what we mean. On July 6, 1607, Duke Christian of Saxony arrived in Prague on a courtesy visit. He stayed a week, during which he was housed in a palace beside and communicating with the imperial residence. His conduct here started tongues wagging and certainly he did not add to his prestige. We shall not dwell on the matter, but shall merely record that the Duke, who was common in appearance and grossly fat, found the opportunity to get drunk six times in seven days, thereby offering a continued and disgusting spectacle of vulgar behavior. What interests us most, however, is that his

[1] *Commentariolum,* in *Opera omnia,* vol. X, pars 2, p. 376.

court preacher, Polycarp Leyser, a theologian highly esteemed by the Lutherans, was among the four hundred members of his retinue. As we have already seen, only two faiths, Catholicism and Hussitism, were then recognized in Bohemia, yet despite this, Leyser preached twice from a window of the palace overlooking a large inner courtyard that was open to the public. These sermons, well advertised in advance, made a great stir both because of the large crowds they drew and because they seemed to be an open provocation to the Catholics.

After the first sermon, Father Larwence wished to take immediate action and offered to refute the Lutheran preacher's errors from the pulpit, but for various reasons the Nuncio was opposed to his doing so. The Saint obeyed, although every fiber of his being cried out for action. However, after Leyser had preached the second time, the Nuncio gave Father Lawrence permission to reply, which he did so energetically, competently, and skillfully that he completely demolished the Lutheran's arguments. Furthermore, in order to discredit Leyser's vaunted knowledge of the Bible, Father Lawrence challenged him publicly to prove that he even knew how to read the Scriptures in the original texts. Although Leyser was still in Prague when Father Lawrence preached against him, he took care not to take up the challenge, but hastened out of the city without saying a word. So it was that Leyser's attempt to increase the glory and prestige of Protestantism in the capital of the empire was turned into a resounding defeat; and his fame never recovered from the rude shock it received at the hands of the saintly Capuchin.

Lutheranismi Hypotyposis

When Leyser returned to his home in Dresden, he published his two sermons in an effort to compensate for his defeat. To the sermons he added an introduction and a conclusion that were really an attack on Father Lawrence and the Jesuits, who had also fought him energetically. Among other things in this attack, Leyser invited his adversaries to reply if they had a spark of honor and were truly sincere. In order the more surely to attain his end, the preacher did his utmost to ensure a wide circulation for his pamphlet in Prague and beyond, even sending a copy to Father Lawrence with a dedication written in his own hand.

The Capuchin could not let such a flagrant provocation pass without comment, and after replying to the pamphlet in a sermon, he set about writing a personal answer or *Apologeticum,* as he entitled it. His reply, however, was not to be so personal as to prevent its being circulated eventually among the people in order to offset the effects produced by the Lutheran's pamphlet. But as he wrote, his original plan began to change and develop. His thoughts turned more and more to the public, for whom in practice he was composing his reply, with the result that he found it necessary to enlarge upon and deal more basically with certain truths and errors. Thus penetrating even further into the subject, he realized that in refuting Leyser's errors, he was really refuting those of Luther, of whom Leyser professed to be a faithful disciple. Hence his reply began to focus more upon the founder of Lutheranism than upon the follower of that heresy.

89

Once he had started on this approach, Father Lawrence continued to pursue it, for he was quickly convinced that it would be better to shift the emphasis from Leyser to Luther, that it would be more worthwhile to combat Leyser through Luther than vice versa; it would be better to concentrate on the master rather than on the disciple, for when the master was defeated, all his disciples would thereby be routed too.

Hence Leyser and his pamphlet ceased to be the Saint's principal target and became only his secondary objective, so that the heretic's attack turned out to be merely the occasion and not the basis of Father Lawrence's work. Taking the pamphlet as his point of departure, the Saint launched a devastating offensive on Lutheranism, refuting it in the most original and ingenious way imaginable. His refutation, under the title *Lutheranismi Hypotyposis,* had three aspects: historical, in which he studied the origin and growth of Protestantism by means of a vivid representation (*hypotyposis*) of the person of its founder, Luther; doctrinal, in which he studied the theory and errors of the heresy in the doctrine of the Lutheran Church; and finally, the practical aspect, in which he used Leyser as an object lesson in Lutheranism as it was in practice and as it affected its adherents.

The most characteristic and ingenious feature of the work was that it combined in a hitherto unknown synthesis all the advantages offered by the various methods followed by previous controversialists; that is to say, it combined the advantages of the historico-personal approach with those of the doctrinal approach. Again, it offered a unified and universal view of Lutheran errors, furnished the arguments to refute them, and set down learned apologetics in a popular form that was really useful to all kinds of people, theologians as well as laymen.

No book of this kind, written in readily understood language and easily consulted, had ever appeared before in the Catholic world, although the lack of such a work had been keenly felt, particularly in places where the faithful had to rub shoulders daily with the innovators. Another great advantage of the book was the author's unparalleled competence in using the originals of those Scripture texts to which the Protestants usually appealed for support. We can truly say that in this regard Father Lawrence's work was a general mobilization of the Bible in a formidable attack upon Luther's position. It would be difficult, not to say impossible, to make a more complete collection of biblical material refuting Protestant errors.

One aspect of the work that particularly impresses the scholar is the scrupulous care with which the author went back to original sources in order to avoid distorting history or misrepresenting his adversaries' doctrine. For example, when he was dealing with Luther's teachings, he was not content to rely upon what others had written and did not quote material at second hand. Instead, he himself checked Luther's works so carefully that it is possible to single out the particular edition and the very pages he consulted. We can see from all this how scientifically and painstakingly Father Lawrence worked.[2]

2 P. Claudio da Solesino, O.F.M.Cap., in his book, *L'apologetica di S. Lorenzo da Brindisi: Originalità,* Roma-Verona, 1959, speaks about the logical development and originality of the *Hypotyposis.*

Unfortunately, the Saint was prevented by the press of events from putting the finishing touches to the book and having it published. We cannot refrain from expressing our regret that such a work as this, which would have been so incalculably useful down through the years, has remained for centuries locked in musty archives, venerated and respected, it is true, but absolutely useless and ignored as far as its real function and importance are concerned.

Chapter VII

The Ambassador

Again Commissary General

IN THE spring of 1608, while the Saint was busy writing his *Hypotyposis,* his confreres in the province of Otranto elected him Vicar Provincial. However, due to a complicated chain of circumstances, the election did not go into effect and Father Lawrence remained in Prague. Since his return to this city, he had had no responsibility except that of preaching in the friary church. But although he did not take part in the General Chapter held in Rome on May 23 of that year, he was elected Commissary General of the Bohemo-Austrian mission and was commissioned to begin the division between it and the newly erected Commissariate of Styria.

The Saint's responsibility as Commissary General, with its accompanying obligation of visiting the friaries twice annually, slowed down his writing of the *Hypotyposis* and distracted him somewhat from his duties as preacher at Prague, an office which he continued to hold. Nevertheless, despite unavoidable interruptions, his congregation grew continually larger and his words were listened to with increasing respect. It was due to his influence that the friary, besides being a center of spirituality, gradually became more and more popular as a meeting place for politicians who would often gather there after the Saint's sermons to ask his advice or to conduct their business safe from prying eyes.

From Bad to Worse

Father Lawrence's prestige grew daily because of the courageous and unrelenting battle he continued to fight against the heretics' maneuverings and also because of his friendship with Maximilian of Bavaria, who was already becoming prominent among the heads of state in Germany and with whom the Saint kept up a continuous personal correspondence. But while the people held him in high esteem for these reasons, they venerated and loved him for the sanctity that shone out in his whole life and particularly in certain unusual events that could only be called miracles.

No wonder then that his words, always so frank and trenchant, and sometimes even prophetic, had great effect. In a voice often broken by sobs, he would speak of the sad and fearful things that threatened the empire and Prague, and his audience would tremble at his prophetic voice and his somber forecast of things to come. Certainly the times were not such as to foster any illusions. Due to Rudolph II's inertia and indifference, the imperial machinery of government had ground to a halt, and the heretics in the Empire, particularly the Calvinists, were becoming increasingly active. The leader of the Calvinist movement, Frederick IV the Elector, aided by the skilled diplomat Christian d'Anhalt, used every effort to spread fear of the power wielded by the Pope, by Spain, and by the Duke of Bavaria, whose quick, decisive action at Donauwörth had impressed the whole of Germany. In this way, Frederick was able to form a secret confederacy of the principal Calvinist states and to lay the foundations for the Evangelical Union, whose object was to defend the real or imaginary rights of its members with an army of twelve thousand men and resist whatever imperial decrees might be prejudicial to their interests. Furthermore, the Union was intended to fight every attempt by Spain or the Pope to help the Catholics and it was particularly dedicated to preventing any Catholic ruler from coming to power in the duchies of Jülich, Cleves, and Berg, which would soon be leaderless.

The Union's first act was to disrupt completely the Diet of Ratisbon which Rudolph II convoked at the beginning of 1608 to collect from the states of the Empire the funds necessary to finance a new offensive against the Turks. A dangerous complication was added to the situation in April of the same year when the Archduke Matthias revolted against his brother, the Emperor, forcing him to surrender to him the provinces of Austria and Moravia and the royal crown of Hungary. This grave discord between the two brothers of the House of Hapsburg increased alarmingly the danger to the Church and the Catholic states of Germany. The heretics in the countries ruled by the Hapsburgs set out to exploit the situation by making arrogant and menacing claims to full freedom of worship, a freedom which they would have soon changed into oppression of the Catholics, as they had done in the past.

But that was not all. Just at this time, the long-expected death of the Duke of Jülich, Cleves, and Berg left vacant the throne of a territory which, lying as it did between France, the Netherlands, and southern Germany, was of supreme political and strategic importance. Neither France nor the heretics wanted a Hapsburg prince as ruler of this wealthy and extensive region. Hence, forestalling any imperial decree, two Calvinist princes, the Elector of Brandenburg and Count Philip of Neuburg, invaded the territory at the beginning of 1609, while the army of the Evangelical Union, becoming daily more threatening, began to carry out raids on the Catholic states of the Rhine.

German Catholicism had never before been in a more precarious position, and many people were already taking a fatalistic view of the march of events. For his part, Father Lawrence, more disturbed yet more inexorable than ever, raised his voice against every compromise and, with the consent of the Nuncio and the Archbishop, organized public prayers and ceremonies of expiation to implore God's mercy. At the same time, however, working secretly with Maximilian, he was making plans for decisive action to remedy the Church's unstable position.

The Catholic League

In view of the progressive worsening of the political situation in the Empire, the Duke of Bavaria had long been trying to make the German Catholic rulers and the Holy See understand the need for a united effort to defend the Faith. So far, his advice had not been favorably received, but now, with the formation of the Evangelical Union, more than one ruler took heed and was ready to join him in a united front against the enemy's threat. This was the union of Catholic rulers that came to be known as the Catholic League.

However, it was clear that without outside assistance

the Catholic confederates would never be a match for the Evangelical Union, which was receiving secret support from France. Hence Maximilian resolved to make an effort to win the Holy See and the King of Spain to the cause of the Catholic League. The gravity of the situation demanded swift and decisive action but, at the same time, the strictest secrecy was necessary so as not to anger the Calvinists more and give them an excuse to become more threatening and arrogant.

Maximilian conferred with the Spanish ambassador at Prague, and both statesmen agreed at once to send Father Lawrence as their envoy to Spain, for, besides possessing sanctity, irresistible powers of persuasion and skill at winning people's loyalty, he was already well known by name to the Spanish royal family.

Thus it was that on June 6, 1609, the saintly Capuchin set out for Munich while, in order to keep his mission secret, a rumor was circulated in Prague that he was returning to Italy by order of the Pope. At Munich he conferred with Maximilian, from whom he received all the necessary instructions. Then crossing the Tyrol and Lombardy, he took ship at Genoa for Spain. Needless to say, he had already obtained, through the Nuncio, the required permissions and recommendations from the Pope.

In the name of Maximilian and the Catholic League, Father Lawrence was to obtain from Philip III an annual subsidy sufficient to maintain two regiments of infantry of three thousand soldiers each and one regiment of cavalry of one thousand five hundred units. The total annual expense would be close to 300,000 ducats or 360,000 scudi, and Philip would have to provide it without any conditions attached. Furthermore, in order to ensure the King's continued support, Father Lawrence was detailed to do his best to persuade him to join the League.

Upon his arrival in Madrid toward the middle of September, the Capuchin set to work without delay and quickly succeeded in winning the favor and confidence of the King, the Queen and the whole court, so that every door was open to him and he could have an audience with the King whenever he chose. Even more than that, the Queen had such a high regard for him that she often had private conferences with him in which the King sometimes joined. The little Prince, the future Philip IV, had a great affection for the Saint and although ill and confined to bed, he wanted to see Father Lawrence every day. And the Saint would visit him daily, bringing him some little gift each time. To crown all this, miracles began to happen, miracles whose authenticity the Capuchin himself acknowledges in letters to Maximilian.[1] Thus helped by his personal prestige and by the favor he found with everyone, he was able, among other things, to overcome the grave difficulties which stood in the way of founding a Capuchin friary in Madrid, and, even more important, he succeeded in surmounting the serious obstacles to obtaining the funds he sought.

The Duke of Lerma, the King's minister, exerted pressure on Philip to impose two conditions for the granting of the funds: first, that the Pope give a sum equal to that given by Spain; and second, that all the Hapsburg princes, or at least the majority of them, enter the Catholic League. These conditions were truly burdensome ones. The Holy See would never have ac-

[1] Letter of October 24, 1609.

Il B. Lorenzo da Brindisi
Gen.le dell' Ord: de Min: Cappuccini
chiaro per Virtù, e Miracoli, morì
l'anno 1619. li 22. Luglio —

ST. LAWRENCE WRITING HIS *Mariale*. (*Engraving by Carlo Baroni. Capuchin Museum, Rome.*)

FAÇADE OF THE CHURCH OF ST. MARY OF THE ANGELS, BRINDISI.

cepted the first, and the second was an implicit yet nonetheless grave expression of distrust of Maximilian of Bavaria, since it would in practice mean taking the leadership of the League from Maximilian and conferring it on a Hapsburg prince, that is, on a prince of the same family as the King of Spain. The fact was that certain ministers in Madrid seemed so concerned about the great prestige Maximilian enjoyed in Germany that they were afraid that if they gave him unconditionally the assistance he asked and allowed him to preside over the League, he would take advantage of the situation to further his own interests and even to supplant the House of Hapsburg on the imperial throne. However, when Father Lawrence remonstrated and protested strongly, the King assured him explicitly and formally that he would give the requested assistance without any conditions and that he himself would join the League.

Having thus fulfilled his mission, the Saint set out at once for Italy and arrived in Rome at the beginning of February, 1610. There at the papal court he found three other ambassadors whom the Duke of Bavaria and the other Catholic leaders had sent to seek financial help from the Pope for the League. Father Lawrence at once joined forces with these envoys.

The nature of this biography prevents us from following these negotiations in detail. Suffice it to say that grave difficulties arose in Rome also, difficulties caused in great part by a sudden reversal of policy by Philip III. More worried than ever by the subtle insinuations and treacherous calumnies which Maximilian's enemies had put into circulation, Philip had deemed it prudent to proceed very cautiously in granting the assistance

103

asked by the League and, going back on the formal promise which he had made to the Duke of Bavaria and Father Lawrence, he had decided to demand the fulfillment of the two conditions suggested by his minister. This radical change of attitude by Philip III gave rise to grave complications that not only slowed down the negotiations but threatened to wreck them.

Maximilian was understandably angered by the turn of events, and in order to provoke him still further, some of his enemies tried to prevent Father Lawrence's return to Germany. Despite everything, however, the Saint arrived in Munich at the end of May after having accompanied the three German ambassadors to the courts of several Italian rulers in an effort to win their support for the League. In Bavaria he found the Duke's rage mounting because Spain had determined to take the command of the League away from him. In fact, Maximilian was so full of resentment that he had decided to withdraw from the confederation and let the others shift for themselves. Yet since a defense organization was unthinkable without the participation of Bavaria, Father Lawrence had to use all his powers of persuasion to remedy the situation. During June, July, and August he acted as courier and ambassador between Munich and Prague with such skill that both parties finally came to a full agreement.

The founding and reinforcement of the League had encouraging repercussions throughout the German Empire. The Evangelical Union, hitherto so arrogant, had to humble itself by asking Maximilian and the Catholic League members for a treaty. Father Lawrence would have preferred not to make any agreement with them, thereby giving the Calvinists a salutary lesson that they would remember. At any rate, the founding of the League and the conclusion of this agreement gave the Catholics of the Empire new heart.

The founding of the League had certainly been a great accomplishment, one which bore the mark of Maximilian's genius but which was also proof of the intuition and skill of another great man who, in many ways, was comparable to Maximilian. That man, of course, was Father Lawrence. It was not without reason, therefore, that Maximilian publicly declared that the whole of Catholic Europe owed Father Lawrence undying gratitude and eternal recognition for his work on behalf of the League.

At Maximilian's Court

Having brought to a successful close his negotiations on behalf of the League, Father Lawrence turned to putting the final touches to the affairs of the Bohemo-Austrian province, of which he was still Commissary General. Then, toward the middle of October, he returned to Munich by order of the Pope, who had acceded to Maximilian's wish to have the Capuchin at his court.

From this point on, the bonds of friendship between the Capuchin and the Duke became even closer than they were before. The Capuchin friary in Munich was situated on a bastion of the city walls and was connected directly with the Duke's palace by an underground passage. Maximilian had always loved to frequent this friary but after Father Lawrence's arrival, he practically lived there. He began by being particularly faithful in attending the Saint's Mass in a private

105

oratory, accompanied by his wife. This Mass, as we shall see later, did not take the usual half hour or so but continued for many hours, a trait to be admired but not imitated. In order to confer with Father Lawrence, the Duke would come to the friary at the most unexpected times, sometimes even in the small hours of the morning. It would not even be an exaggeration to say that during all the time that Father Lawrence was in Munich, that is until the spring of 1613, there was no business, public or private, religious or political, great or small, about which the Duke did not consult his friend and spiritual director.

The Capuchin's presence at Maximilian's side during this period when Bavaria was growing in importance and becoming the pivotal point of the Catholic defences in Germany, soon revealed itself as truly providential. In his capacity as Apostolic Nuncio, although he had not been officially proclaimed as such, the Saint kept up a regular diplomatic correspondence with the representatives of the Holy See. The information which he diligently and regularly supplied them was all the more valuable because the Duke of Bavaria, by means of a tightly woven net of correspondents and agents, was always kept up to the minute as to what was happening all over Germany and abroad.

While the Saint's presence in Munich was useful and providential for the Holy See, it was none the less so for Maximilian himself. Thanks to the authority and influence which he had with the Duke, Father Lawrence was able on several occasions to soothe the anger of his hot-headed friend, as happened, to cite only one example, in the serious dispute in 1611 with the Archbishop of Salzburg, Wolfgang Theodoric von Raitenau. Because the Duke claimed the right to collect certain tolls, relations between him and the Archbishop had already been rather strained for several years, but in 1611 the situation came to a head when the fiery prelate took counter-measures that infringed gravely on the Duke's prerogatives and interests. At the urgent recommendation of the Holy See itself, Father Lawrence did all he could to avert the worst, but when the Archbishop threw caution to the winds and took up arms, the Capuchin could not prevent Maximilian from following suit, invading the archdiocese and occupying Salzburg. It was well that, during the Duke's military expedition, the Saint remained at his side to cool his anger and pacify him as best he could, for in the months that followed Father Lawrence's continuous, discreet influence was instrumental in restoring to normal the relations between the Duke and the Holy See. Fully aware of the Saint's efficacy as a mediator and a restraining influence on him, Maximilian continually strove to have the Holy See allow Father Lawrence to remain with him, and hitherto he had been successful. It was not until the beginning of 1612, after the death of Rudolph II, when King Matthias began to enter the political scene with his powerful minister, Melchior Klesl, that the pontifical authorities considered recalling Father Lawrence from Germany. Klesl was an avowed enemy of Bavaria, and the whole of Austria was becoming increasingly fearful and jealous of the Duke's power. And since, as everyone knew, Father Lawrence was not only Maximilian's friend but also his ardent champion and admirer, Klesl wanted to have him removed from Munich. The Saint himself was in full agreement with the Austrian minister on this point, for, ready and willing as he was to make any sacrifice for the good of the Church, he was suffering greatly from his ailments and longed to return to the gentler climate of his own country.

Hence when he went to Rome for the General Chapter in the spring of 1613, he was kept in Italy. It is worth noting, however, that being treated as an enemy by a statesman such as Klesl, who was crafty, Machiavellian and too accommodating to the Protestants, was by no means detrimental to the Saint's reputation. On the contrary, Klesl's opposition was a new honor and a further proof that his diplomatic endeavors had been completely opposed to any compromise with the enemy and directed exclusively toward the benefit of the Church and the faithful.

Missionary Work

Father Lawrence's diplomatic activity, although it was the most obvious, was not the only work he did in Munich. First of all, he had to act as Commissary General of the Bavarian-Tyrolean province from 1611 to 1612 because the plague had prevented the Chapter from meeting to carry out the regular annual elections. Furthermore, besides his almost continuous application to exercises of piety, he preached frequently in the friary church and often had the Duke and Duchess of Bavaria in his congregation. But even all of that did not satisfy his apostolic zeal. Whenever circumstances and his health permitted, he courageously undertook veri-

108

table missionary expeditions not merely into Catholic
territory but also among the heretics. These expeditions
were not without danger, even grave danger, and sometimes armed attempts on his life were made. Yet no
peril or threat could intimidate him, for he longed for
martyrdom as the highest of rewards.

Chapter VIII

The Peacemaker

Vicar Provincial of Genoa

A T THE General Chapter of 1613, Father Lawrence was elected for a third term as Definitor General and was sent as visitator to the province of Liguria-Piedmont, where things were not as they should be. At this period Liguria and Piedmont belonged to different states, Liguria being subject to the republic of Genoa and traditionally allied to Spain, while Piedmont, under the Duke of Savoy, had completely opposite tendencies. The differences of opinion caused by these diverse political affiliations had appeared even in the friaries, where the religious lived together without any distinction of nationality. While these divergent loyalties had caused no discord among the main body of the friars, a minority of the Piedmontese had resolved to break off from the Genoese at all costs and form a separate province.

There is no doubt that the Piedmontese friars had serious reasons for wanting the change. But they were wrong in the methods they used to attain their end, for they had recourse to the support and intervention of Charles Emmanuel I, Duke of Savoy, nor did they scruple to raise doubts in his mind, doubts that were actually justified, as to the loyalty of their Genoese confreres. Hence, solely for political reasons, Charles Emmanuel began to support his subjects' cause with

113

resolute tenacity, insisting energetically that every "foreigner" be removed from his territory.

Naturally, the Capuchin superiors could not yield to such a demand or tolerate the Duke's interference in the affairs of the Order, all the less so because other rulers declared explicitly that if the Duke was given satisfaction they would demand that the same measures be put into effect in their territories. Hence the Chapter of 1613 was unwilling to divide the province of Liguria-Piedmont along the lines demanded by Charles Emmanuel, but instead sent Father Lawrence there as Visitator General. When the Saint had made the visitation he went to Turin to negotiate with the Duke, but Charles Emmanuel would not listen to reason and treated the Capuchin with open contempt. However, to the ruler's great chagrin, Father Lawrence broke off the negotiations, left Turin immediately and went to Pavia, where he had arranged to hold the provincial Chapter on September 13. Despite his expressed wishes, this Chapter elected him Vicar Provincial almost unanimously and, disregarding his immediate protests, the members of the Chapter intoned the *Te Deum* as they went to the church in procession for the customary ceremony. The Saint could do nothing but resign himself to his fate and join in the procession.

Meanwhile, Charles Emmanuel, more angered than ever at not getting what he wanted, took the reprisals that he had long threatened. He informed Father Lawrence, as the new Provincial, that he would no longer tolerate "foreigners" in his territory and that, consequently, all the Genoese would have to leave Piedmont. He further decreed that he would not even allow "foreign" superiors to visit their subjects in future, and he warned Father Lawrence to take good care not to set foot in the ducal territory again. The Saint had already suspected how the affair would end and he had no difficulty in adapting himself to the new circumstances. Yet he knew that the Duke needed little further excuse to expel all the Capuchins from Piedmont. This dispute with Charles Emmanuel and the troublesome behavior of a certain group of religious caused Father Lawrence continuous pain during his three years as provincial.

In June, 1615, the Vicar General of the Order, giving in to the Duke's importunate appeals to the superiors, the cardinals, and even the Pope, called together in Rome the Definitors General, including Father Lawrence. After re-examining the question, all were very firmly agreed not to make any changes and not to give Charles Emmanuel any satisfaction. They had no intention of tolerating the intrusion of secular rulers into the affairs of the Order.

As if to console the Saint for so many troubles, the people of Liguria lavished upon him their unlimited devotion and esteem. Everywhere he went they pressed around him to see him, to touch him, and to get his blessing; and many miracles were performed. On his part, Father Lawrence exhorted them to live better lives, as he preached in the churches of the villages and in the cathedrals of the towns through which he passed. In 1614 he gave the Lenten sermons in the cathedral of Genoa and, in 1615, in the ducal chapel at Santa Barbara in Mantua.

Among Father Lawrence's accomplishments on behalf of the people of Liguria there is one which deserves special mention, if only briefly. At this time the coastal town of Oneglia belonged to the Duke of Savoy, but in November, 1614, the Spaniards, who were at war with the Duke, decided to take it away from him. With the permission of the republic of Genoa, they disembarked close by, at Portomaurizio, and laid siege to the town. The Piedmontese fought bravely but without any hope of success, while, as so often occurs, the noncombatants had to bear the consequences. Father Lawrence, who fortunately happened to be in the district, offered to negotiate a surrender in order to alleviate the people's sufferings and put an end to the devastation of the siege. He succeeded in doing so, although only with difficulty.

With the Troops

Tired of being superior, dogged by pain and ill-health, and harassed especially by the continual cares of his office as Provincial of Genoa, Father Lawrence looked forward with relief to the approach of the provincial Chapter that was to be held at Pavia on August 2, 1616, with Father Paul of Cesena, the Vicar General, presiding. But when he went to meet Father Paul in Piacenza at the end of July, he fell so gravely ill that his life was endangered. When the Duke of Parma, Ranuccio Farnese I, heard of the Saint's illness, he did everything possible to help him, sending his best specialists and providing the most costly medicines. But when Ranuccio saw that, despite everything, Father Lawrence's condition continued to grow worse and that there was little hope for recovery, he made elaborate arrangements so that if the Saint died, his body would not be taken away. The Duke even obtained from the

116

INTERIOR OF THE CHURCH OF ST. MARY OF THE ANGELS, BRINDISI.

La Nobiltà Napolitana supplica S. Lorenzo da Brindisi per una ambasceria di Filippo III contro il Duca di Ossuna
(Da un quadro a tempra del Monti)

THE NEAPOLITAN NOBLES BEGGING ST. LAWRENCE TO BE THEIR AMBASSADOR TO PHILIP III. (*By E. Polizzi, from a painting by Del Monti. Capuchin Museum, Rome.*)

Vicar General the explicit promise that, besides the Saint's body, everything that he had with him at the time of his death would remain in the Duke's possession.

Father Lawrence had already received Viaticum with tears of devotion, and the end seemed near, when a totally unexpected change in his condition occurred and he began to recover rapidly. Indeed, so quickly did he regain his strength that in a short time he was able to leave for Pavia, where the provincial Chapter was held on August 16, two weeks late.

Freed from all responsibility, the Saint would have liked to set out at once for his own province of Venice, where he hoped to spend a few peaceful years at long last. But Cardinal Ludovisi, the Papal Legate assigned to negotiating for peace between Spain and the Duke of Savoy, wanted to make use of the Saint's diplomatic skill. Consequently he asked him to present himself to the Spanish governor, Don Pedro de Toledo, in an effort to persuade him to accept an eventual arrangement. The Saint had no choice but to do as the Cardinal requested.

Don Pedro was encamped near Candia Lomellina, ready to launch an attack on the Savoyard troops deployed along the other side of the Sesia. But while Father Lawrence was carrying out his mission, the Savoyards took the initiative, attacked the Spaniards, and laid an ambush for them near Candia. At once, the Saint left negotiations aside and thought only of helping the soldiers. As before in Hungary, he did not hesitate to go to the front lines, encouraging and reassuring the troops by his presence and blessings. In the end, victory went to the Spaniards, a victory which Don Pedro and his soldiers attributed solely to Father Lawrence.

Calm Interlude

After this eventful period, the Saint set out to travel to Verona by easy stages, and, after stopping at Parma and Mantua, he finally arrived at his destination in the latter part of December, 1616. He remained there until spring of the following year, meanwhile preaching the Sunday Lenten sermons in the friary church. This was a brief interlude of peace and spiritual joy for him despite his intense physical sufferings and the importunity of the devout populace, all of whom wanted to see him and get his blessing.

In April he went to Venice, where his confreres received him with great joy. Not only the Venetian aristocracy but even the Doge himself came to visit him, and growing crowds began to besiege him, clamoring for his miraculous blessing. The enthusiasm of the people was still increasing when, toward the middle of June, he passed through Padua on his way to the friary at Bassano del Grappa. There, on the mountainside at the edge of the vast plain of Padua, he was able to spend seven long months in peace, surrounded by the affection and veneration of his confreres.

"The Sweat of Death"

The peace of his stay at Bassano was rudely broken by an order from Rome at the beginning of February, 1618, commanding him to start at once for Milan to meet the Spanish governor, Don Pedro de Toledo, whom he was to persuade to make peace with the Duke of Savoy and to restore to him the fortress of Vercelli which had been captured about a year before.

Although hard pressed on all sides, the governor could not bring himself to take this final step, always finding new pretexts for avoiding it. He let it be understood that, among other things, he wanted to speak first with Father Lawrence, for whom he had boundless esteem. The Saint arrived in Milan in the latter part of March and, as a result of his skill, prestige, and sanctity, he succeeded where so many others had failed. Later Don Pedro would say it was solely as a result of Father Lawrence's advice and persuasion that he decided to give Vercelli back to Savoy.

While the Saint's presence in Milan was very agreeable to Don Pedro, and very useful for the cause of peace, it was not so pleasant for his confreres, because his being there robbed them of all quiet since he attracted such crowds that the situation became insupportable. There wasn't a corner left in which the friars could take refuge and find a little peace, for the cloister, the garden, the church and the neighboring streets swarmed with people, nobles and commoners alike, so much so that the whole affair began to assume the proportions of a disaster. Finally, the religious decided that the only remedy was to send the Saint out of Milan to the friary at Melzo. But when after a few days the governor had him recalled to the city, the friars were forced to insist that he be allowed to return to Venice.

Toward the middle of April, the Saint was again in Bassano, and shortly thereafter he left finally to attend the provincial Chapter that was to be held in Padua on April 27. Meanwhile, the General Chapter was approaching and he had already done all he could to avoid having to attend it. On January 19 he had written to his friend Father Remigio of Bozzolo: "The thought of having to leave this solitude to plunge into such a sea of distractions causes me to break out in the sweat of death." But despite his repugnance and difficulties, the Vicar General and the Procurator of the Order had placed on him the obligation to attend, so that he had to resign himself to doing so.

But there was something more than "a sea of distractions" to cause him to fall into "the sweat of death." "Brother Ambrose," he said to a dear friend as he set out from Padua for Rome, "Brother Ambrose, we shall never see each other again." Then he added, "Pray for me," [1] for he felt the chill of approaching death.

To Naples

His journey to Rome, like his return from Milan, was a triumphal procession through Italy, although for the Saint himself it was really a road to Calvary. His travelling companion, Brother Giammaria of Monteforte, has left us a description which shows us what almost unbelievable heights the people's devotion and enthusiasm reached as the Saint journeyed south through Rovigo, Ferrara, Rimini, Loreto, Foligno and Spoleto.

Father Lawrence was re-elected Definitor General at the Chapter and remained only a short time in Rome because the Duke of Bavaria, with whom he corresponded continually, had asked him to go to Brindisi to visit the Church of St. Mary of the Angels and the adjoining convent of Capuchin nuns which he, the Duke, had had built on the site of the Saint's home.

Leaving Rome about the middle of July, at the height

[1] Deposition of P. Ambrogio da Firenze, in *Proc. Ap. Ven.,* pars I, f. 196v.

of the summer, he arrived several days later at Naples, where, on the advice of the General, he remained, to allow the worst of the heat to pass. Needless to say, when he reached Naples, the crowds were even larger and more enthusiastic than elsewhere. Indeed, the poor friars were sometimes at their wit's end as to how to ward them off.

Chapter IX

The Lover of the Eucharist and of Mary

WE HAVE just mentioned the Church of St. Mary of the Angels and the convent of the Capuchin nuns. When Father Lawrence had passed through Brindisi in 1604 during his term as General, he had realized the need for a new and more suitable residence for the Capuchin nuns, who until then had been living in the Convent of St. Clare opposite the cathedral. The authorities at Brindisi had been the first to take an interest in building a new convent, but later, either because of disagreement with the ecclesiastical authorities or because of lack of means, construction had been suspended. It was at this juncture that Father Lawrence came to the nuns' assistance.

Upon his return to Germany in 1606, he had set about collecting the necessary funds from various princes, and, out of esteem for the Saint, the Duke of Bavaria had undertaken the complete construction of a convent on the site of his friend's old home. The building was finished in 1618, and the church was endowed with a veritable treasure of relics and sacred furnishings.

The edifice was not only a proof of Maximilian's affection and esteem for Father Lawrence but also a witness to the Saint's love for his native city. Above all it was and still is a testimony to his great love for the

127

Mother of God: it was not without reason that he wished the church to be dedicated to St. Mary of the Angels, like the first little church at Assisi, which had served as the cradle of the Franciscan Order, and like the humble Capuchin church at Venice which he had frequented while he was still a child.

Before we finish this short biography of the Saint, we must speak, if only briefly, about his boundless love for the Mother of God, a love which was such an outstanding feature of his spiritual life that it merits special attention. Devotion to Mary was so deeply rooted in the Saint's heart that it became a part of him and exercised a profound and mysterious influence on his whole life. Indeed, it seemed to be a sort of supernatural instinct, and it appeared to have become, like all instincts, connatural to his very being.

Those who lived with him were apparently unable to find words to describe his devotion to Mary. His confrere and travelling companion, Brother Giammaria of Monteforte, declared that "the devotion which Father Lawrence of Brindisi always bore for the Blessed Virgin was boundless and so great that I cannot express it. As far as I could see, all his thoughts and affections were directed to the Mother of God, after God himself. She was the joy and happiness of his heart." [1]

His devotion to Mary was permeated with gratitude, for he was completely convinced that he had received everything from her and through her. He had been born on a Saturday, Mary's day, and he attributed his very existence to her. To her also he attributed his vocation and the grace of having received a favorable acceptance at the end of the novitiate; his cure during the course of

[1] *Proc. Ap. Mil.,* p. 735.

128

his studies and, consequently, the grace of the priesthood and the apostolate; the victory at Alba Regalis, for
he had given the troops the two names of "Jesus, Mary"
as a countersign; all his knowledge and particularly his
perfect command of Hebrew; and, finally, the grace of
being free from temptation to sensuality. In short, he
felt that he owed everything to her and he was not
afraid to proclaim his indebtedness from the pulpit. For
the rest, no one affirmed Mary's universal mediation
with more assurance than he: "Every gift, every grace,
every good that we have and that we receive continually, we receive through Mary. If Mary did not exist,
neither would we, nor would the world." [2]

Experience had taught him to leave the future completely in Mary's hands and to abandon himself to her
heavenly protection as a child in its mother's arms. He
wanted all Christians to have the same full and limitless
confidence and he proclaimed aloud that "God wants
everyone, *everyone,* to learn this truth from childhood
on—that he who trusts in Mary, that he who relies on
Mary, will never be abandoned either in this world or
the next." [3]

He himself always trusted in the Blessed Virgin,
abandoning himself to her motherly protection, especially in the most important and decisive moments of
his life. For example, just after his election as General,
he went to Loreto first before beginning his heroic
journey on foot across Europe. Again, in 1607, he confided to Mary's protection the outcome of his contro-
versy with Leyser, the Lutheran theologian. His love of
Our Lady found moving expression in the traditional

[2] Munich, *Hof-u. Staatsbibliothek, Cod. it.* 335, f. 154r.
[3] *Ibid.* f. 158r.

forms of Marian devotion that had always been prac-
ticed in the Franciscan Order, such as the Rosary and
the Office of the Blessed Virgin. Often as he walked
through the verdant countryside and over the flowering
hills he would become a troubador like St. Francis and
"would sing songs of praise to the Blessed Virgin, especially Petrarch's *Vergine bella*." [4] Or he would sing
the *Stabat Mater* or the *Litany of Loreto*. All of this he
would do "with so much feeling that very often he was
taken out of himself, and the strength of his emotion
gave him a lump in the throat that forced him to inter-
rupt his singing until he had regained his self-control." [5]

In order to have, as it were, the physical sensation of
Mary's presence, he always had his travelling companion
carry with him a small picture of the Blessed Virgin
with the Child in her arms. Wherever they halted or
lodged, this picture was given the place of honor and he
often gazed on it with tears in his eyes. He always
stopped at shrines of Our Lady, even going far out of
his way to visit them. His favorite shrine was Loreto,
and whenever he was leaving Rome or returning thereto,
the little house of Our Lady drew him irresistibly.

Besides these manifestations of his love for Mary, he
also performed other acts of devotion to her throughout
his life. From the time of his youth, it was his unvarying
practice to fast every Saturday and on the vigil of each
of Our Lady's feasts. This fast of his was an extremely
rigorous one, and he observed it even when he was ill.
It can truly be said that he always had Mary's name in

[4] Deposition of P. Ambrogio da Firenze, in *Proc. Ap. Ven.*,
pars I, f. 183r.
[5] *Ibid.*

GENERAL VIEW OF THE CONVENT OF THE DISCALCED FRAN-
CISCAN SISTERS AT VILLAFRANCA DEL BIERZO, SPAIN.

his heart and on his lips. Everything reminded him of her. Upon seeing a child in its mother's arms, "he would become very joyful and would caress the baby, saying 'Oh, my dear little one! Oh, my dear little one!' then as he went on his way, he would remain silent for some time, and very often on these occasions he was seen to weep." [6] To him, saying Mary's name was more spontaneous even than breathing, so much so that one of his confreres testfied that "almost every word he said was accompanied by her name." [7] The ejaculation, *Nos cum prole pia benedicat Virgo Maria,* was particularly dear to him. He always repeated it at the end of the community prayers, he often said it in private while at the same time making the sign of the cross over his heart,

[6] *Ibid.,* f. 184v.

[7] Deposition of P. Santo da Gazoldo, in *Proc. Ap. Ven.,* pars II, f. 396v.

131

BEATUS LAURENTIUS A BRUNDUSIO GENERALIS CAPUCINORU
catholicæ pietatis studio Philippo III Hispaniarum ac Siciliarum Regi suadet, ut cæ
Germaniæ Principibus pro tuenda religione adversus impios fœderetur.
Æneas theatrum regit.

ST. LAWRENCE AT THE COURT OF PHILIP III OF SPAIN. (*An engraving by Canego from a picture by I. Ribera, "Spagnoletto."*)

or he wrote it at the end of his letters. Even the blessings which he so often gave the people were not infrequently given in the name of Mary.

As the years passed, his devotion to and love for the Blessed Virgin became more profound and moving. We are told that "He reached the point where, in his last years, whenever he heard anyone speak of God or His Holy Mother, he was immediately taken out of himself and enraptured to such a degree that . . . he remained thus absorbed for periods of full fifteen minutes at a time." [8] In short, devotion to Mary was truly the atmosphere in which he lived and had his being as a saint.

The Mariale

Completely captivated by love of the Blessed Virgin, the Saint lost no opportunity to spread devotion to her. He spoke of her in private conversations and in his many sermons. Other Lenten preachers did not usually preach on Saturdays, but, from the first years of his ministry, he took advantage of the day to preach on Mary. We have already described how, during the Lent of 1605 in Naples, he spoke twice each day so as to be able to preach more on the Blessed Virgin, his morning sermon being concerned with the Gospel of the day and the evening one being devoted to the Hail Mary.

Today we are still able to enjoy the fruit of his sermons and long meditations on Our Lady in his incomparable work, the *Mariale*. No one but a saint consumed with seraphic love for the purest and most perfect of creatures could have written such a book. The

[8] Deposition of Fra' Giammaria da Monteforte, in *Proc. Ap. Mil.*, p. 736.

Mariale, with its eighty-four discourses covering close to six hundred printed pages, is certainly one of the most remarkable pieces of Marian literature ever penned. It is a profound theological treatise on Mary, written, it is true, in oratorical style, but none the less rich, solid and complete for all that. What it lacks in systematic approach, it makes up for in artistic genius, charming presentation and moving fervor. There is no Marian dogma, privilege or subject which Father Lawrence does not discuss, illustrate, and defend. He always writes without empty rhetoric or pious exaggeration, allowing us to sense, behind the orator, the profound theologian ever vigilant and ever sure of his ground. The result is that there is nothing in his book that the most demanding theologian would hesitate to accept and approve.

With great skill he made a synthesis, often filling in the gaps, of all that apologists, theologians and ascetical authors had written before him. At the center of his Mariology, he placed Our Lady's universal motherhood and by the principles of suitability, analogy, eminence, and singularity, he showed how all the privileges and prerogatives that make Mary the wonder of the universe are derived from it. To support his statements and theses, he gave many ingenious and poetic proofs and arguments which he developed himself or found in tradition or, very often, drew from the inexhaustible treasure of Scripture. As we have already seen, his *Hypotyposis Lutheranismi* was a mobilization of the whole Bible against Protestantism; in the same way his *Mariale* was a gathering of the forces of Scripture to the defense and praise of the Mother of God.

134

Perhaps here more than anywhere else we see how Father Lawrence was inspired by Holy Scripture, thought with Holy Scripture, and expressed himself in the language of Holy Scripture. All the accepted interpretations of the Scriptures—literal, typical and accommodated—are here intertwined, complementing each other in a wonderful symphony in honor of the Blessed Virgin, a symphony that sparkles with innumerable biblical images, names, and references. And more wonderful still is the natural and spontaneous way in which each thought and each word flows from the mind and heart and pen of the author. Moreover, the reader is fascinated and won over completely by the fervent love for Mary that runs through and impregnates the whole book from beginning to end. But how could it be otherwise in view of the burning love for the Mother of God that consumed Father Lawrence's heart? It is not surprising, then, that the appearance of the *Mariale* was greeted with a great wave of enthusiasm and praise, or that one writer did not hesitate to say, "This is the best and most complete [treatise] ever written on the Virgin Mother of God." [9]

The Wonder of the Mass

In St. Lawrence we find devotion to Mary closely bound up with devotion to the Eucharist, particularly to the Holy Sacrifice of the Mass. It was precisely for

[9] P. Romualdo Bizarri, O.F.M.Cap. Cf. Hieronymus a Fellette, O.F.M.Cap., *De S. Laurentii a Brundusio Ordinis Minorum Capuccinorum activitate apostolica ac operibus testimoniorum elenchus*, Venetiis, 1937, p. 259.

the purpose of being able to say Mass at his own pace and to take all the time he wanted that in 1618 he hastened away from Rome after the General Chapter. When he arrived in Naples, he wrote to the Duke of Bavaria: "[Now] I can stay at the altar for many hours . . . so that I am almost satisfied." [10] It seems that he was really fully satisfied, for he spent the greater part of the day offering the Holy Sacrifice. From his youth, he had always had special devotion to the Mass, but it was particularly after his term of office as Vicar General that he began to devote all his energy to it and to make it the center, not only of his spiritual life, but also of his whole existence. At first he had taken no more than half an hour to say Mass, but later he began to spend more and more time at the altar. After his return to Prague in 1606, his usual half-hour for Mass quickly became an hour, then two, three and four hours. Perhaps he would have liked to have spent even longer but the limits imposed by the prescriptions of the liturgy prevented him. Furthermore, the length of time he took to say Mass was, to say the least, causing wondering comment among the friars. Hence when he came to Rome in 1610 on behalf of the Catholic League, he obtained from the Pope all the indults and dispensations needed to allow him to avoid causing comment and to spend as long as he liked at Mass. He could now begin the Holy Sacrifice at any hour of the night, he could spend as long in saying it as he wished and, to satisfy his devotion to Our Lady, he had an indult to say her Mass every day except on the principal feasts of the Church.

When he re-crossed the Alps and took up residence in Munich, he began to say the protracted Masses that

[10] Letter of July 27, 1618.

136

became the wonder of all who assisted at them. Now freed from all restrictions, liturgical or otherwise, he prolonged his Masses to six, eight, even ten hours and more. On certain feasts, particularly those of Our Lady, he seemed to be unable to tear himself away from the altar. We are told that, in Naples, in 1618, on the Assumption of Our Lady, he spent fourteen hours saying Mass, and in Genoa at Christmas of the same year he remained sixteen hours, three quarters of the day and night, at the altar.

However, there was another element in his life even more astounding. We have already mentioned the Saint's illnesses several times. Especially after being Vicar General, he began to suffer from increasingly severe arthritic pains in his hands, legs, and feet. Soon he was reduced to such a plight that when the pains attacked him he was not even able to hold a pen or put his foot to the ground and he found the lightest touch intolerably painful. Under such conditions, getting out of bed and saying Mass seemed completely out of the question, but Father Lawrence did just that although he was unable to move or walk and had to be carried to the altar. There his confreres arranged the bandages on his hands so as to leave his fingers sufficiently free to handle the Sacred Species. When the time came to put on the vestments, he seemed to gather strength from some mysterious and unlooked-for source so that he was able to stand up and begin Mass. Not only that, but even when he did not remain at the altar for his usual eight, ten or twelve hours, he still spent a considerable time, about three hours, in offering the Holy Sacrifice— a phenomenon which left those who saw it speechless with wonder. Yet, immediately after Mass, his pains

137

would return and his confreres would have to hasten to hold him up and carry him back to bed.

Once when he was suffering a painful attack, one of the friars advised him not to say Mass but he answered that his pains decreased while he was at the altar. They must have decreased, yet he still suffered atrociously and sometimes he was deathly pale when he finished Mass. Once he let slip a revealing thought by saying, "I really feel as if I'm going to die."

Despite all this, however, his whole bearing gave unmistakable proof that he enjoyed great spiritual consolations which more than counterbalanced his appalling sufferings. Sometimes after the secret prayers of the Mass and especially after the Elevation, he became completely motionless and enraptured. At other times the emotions that surged within his heart were so great that they had to find expression. Then his sighs and moans, his exclamations and invocations, his cries of love and sorrow, of joy or tenderness, became so vehement and so irrepressible that they could be heard at a great distance. On such occasions, he shed so many tears that he had to use two, three, five, six, or even more handkerchiefs to dry them. In the words of one writer, he gave the impression that he was about "to melt away and dissolve like wax in the heat of the sun." [11] Naturally, he used to say Mass in private chapels in order to be more at liberty to follow the urgings of his heart. When he had to say Mass in public, he tried to control his fervor and not lose all sense of time, but he was

---

[11] Iacobilli, G. B. *Sommario della vita del Molto R. Padre F. Lorenzo da Brindisi predicatore cappuccino morto l'anno 1619,* ed. by P. G. Crisostomo da Cittadella, O.F.M.Cap., Verona, 1948, p. 14.

not always successful in this. We shall not pause to
enumerate other very significant events that used to
take place during the Saint's Masses, such as appari-
tions and similar supernatural and mystical manifestations. We think we have said enough to show that when
Father Lawrence was at the altar he seemed to be a
living miracle.

Chapter X

The Enemy of Oppression

WE HAVE seen how Father Lawrence had hastened to leave Rome for Naples with the idea of returning to Brindisi to visit the church of St. Mary of the Angels and to be at liberty to celebrate Mass in peace. But all this has diverted us from our chronological account of his busy life, which we shall now resume.

Arriving in Naples, toward the middle of July, 1618, he remained there, waiting for the heat of the summer to decrease enough to allow him to resume his journey to Brindisi. However, an attack of arthritic pain which "overwhelmed and tortured him atrociously" [1] forced him to delay his departure still more, so that it was not until the latter part of September that he was able to travel again. The next stage of his journey took him to Caserta, where new and unforeseen events prevented him from going farther.

Since 1616, the Kingdom of Naples had been ruled by the Spanish viceroy, Don Pedro Girón, Duke of Osuna, a man who, while he certainly had many good qualities, also had many grave defects of character. Completely dominated by his lower passions and his

[1] Letter of St. Lawrence to the Duke of Bavaria, Oct. 1, 1618.

vaulting ambition, he was capable of every excess, the more so because, as a relative of the Duke of Uceda, who was a great favorite of Philip III, he had such influence that he had nothing to fear from the court at Madrid.

As governor of Sicily from 1610 to 1616, he had already won considerable renown but had also committed great wrongs. The Holy See had not looked with favor on this "thoughtless hothead's" being transferred from the governorship of Sicily to that of Naples, which was more important and nearer the center of things. As a matter of fact, Don Pedro's pugnacity did grow in proportion to the greater importance of his new territory. Formerly he had contented himself with fitting out, on his own initiative, several galleons to keep the Turks in hand, but now he took it upon himself to put a check to the Venetians. The Venetians, besides maintaining less than cordial relations with Spain, had gone to war with Archduke Ferdinand of Graz, who had encouraged the privateers of the Adriatic. Ferdinand, as we know, was a prince of the House of Hapsburg, and to touch a Hapsburg was to touch Spain.

The Duke of Osuna's hostility toward Venice had not diminished after the general peace treaty of 1617. In fact his continual harassment of the Venetians, particularly on the sea, kept Italian politics in a constant turmoil and distressed the Pope and the other princes who wanted a little peace at last. But the Duke was not concerned with peace; what he wanted was a war in which he could humble his rivals. He had found supporters for his nefarious projects in the Marquis of Bedmar, who was the Spanish ambassador in Venice, and in Don Pedro de Toledo, the governor of Milan. But even after these two partners of his had withdrawn from the Italian political scene, Osuna had continued to stir up trouble by keeping his war fleet in a state of readiness and by constantly recruiting new troops. Consequently when Father Lawrence arrived in Naples in the latter part of July, 1618, the Duke had no less than fifteen thousand soldiers under his command, a considerable army that had to be supported. But where was the money to come from?

An Explosive Situation

To Osuna's insistent demands for funds, Madrid replied by repeatedly ordering him to disband his army and disarm his galleons. But he always found a way to avoid carrying out the order. For their part, the Venetians set out to cool the Duke's fervor for war by waylaying Spanish ships in the Adriatic and by making it increasingly difficult for him to obtain supplies. In addition, the bankers became less and less willing to lend him money. Hence, in order to raise funds, the Duke had recourse to the convenient method of levying taxes, of confiscation and extortion, principally at the expense of the aristocracy.

As we would expect, discontent spread and became acute, creating a dangerous situation. In order to control the unfolding of events without changing his basic policy, Osuna stirred up discord and quarrels between the nobles and the people and then openly championed the people's cause at the expense of the nobles. Thus two factions soon formed in Naples, the Osunians and the anti-Osunians, with the Duke expecting to use their antagonism toward each other to further his interests. Meanwhile his real supporters were few and not of very high moral calibre, consisting as they did of a group of barons won over by favors or coerced by threats, and an unruly minority of the citizens of Naples.

There was no likelihood that the inhabitants of other towns or localities would side with the Duke since his troops, billeted in towns and villages throughout the kingdom, were a severe drain on the finances of the individual communities. In fact, in order to meet the enormous expense of supporting the troops, local authorities had to impose ruthless taxes and levies on the people, often reducing them to famine and despair. Worse still, the soldiers, who were accustomed to violence and the use of arms, thought that the longer they were left unpaid, the more they were at liberty to pillage and extort. Appealing to Osuna against these wrongs was useless and even dangerous because he never took sides against his soldiers, for he valued his popularity with his troops more than anything in the world. Hence anyone who was even a little too insistent in making complaints about them was sure to end up behind bars. Having no other means of redressing their wrongs, a growing number of people took to the hills and, by means of ambushes and surprise attacks, dealt out their own justice for the soldiers' depredations. Thus, on both sides, murders and reprisals multiplied.

Then there was the moral aspect of the situation. There was no place where women and families were safe from the violence of the swarms of undisciplined and often drunken soldiers, a fact which only served to increase the people's anger and spur them on to further acts of revenge. The situation was equally disturbing from the religious point of view. Many of the soldiers were foreigners, and in the various companies of French, Walloon, and Scottish mercenaries there were Calvinists, Lutherans and Huguenots, who more than once were guilty of profaning holy places and sacred images, thus arousing the just anger of the people. Needless to say, there was also the very real danger that centers of heretical propaganda would be set up here and there throughout the kingdom.

The likelihood of a general revolt was increased by the fact that during August and September of 1618 the news began to circulate that the Duke, not knowing where to send his soldiers next, was thinking of stationing them in Naples. But by ancient privilege this city was exempt from such an imposition, and the citizens began to protest vehemently. Popular indignation and the danger of an uprising grew greater as the troops actually did begin to move toward the capital.

The nobles, too, were enraged by the Duke's hostile attitude toward them and even more by the diabolical skill or brute force with which he gained entry to their homes and besmirched the honor of even the most distinguished families. In giving rein to his passions, Osuna did not respect even the holiest places, such as churches and convents. Not only that, but his lackeys were almost as exempt from punishment as he himself.

Such was the tragic state of affairs which Father Lawrence found upon his arrival in Naples in the latter part of 1618.

Ambassador of Naples

The anti-Osunist nobles finally decided to take advantage of the general unrest to attack the Duke's position. For a long time past, Osuna had been maneuvering to get the King of Spain to reconfirm him as viceroy since his term of office was coming to an end. But the nobles, intent on preventing his reappointment, resolved to inform Philip III about the very serious state of affairs in the kingdom of Naples and they proposed to accomplish their purpose by sending an ambassador to the court of Madrid. This right of embassy, which served as a check on the viceroy's power, was theirs by ancient privilege.

They began by approaching Osuna himself with a petition that he disband the troops that were scourging the capital and laying waste the whole kingdom. The Duke, however, was unwilling and indeed unable to disperse his army because he hadn't money to pay off their arrears in wages. Yet on the other hand, he did not want to antagonize and stir up the people still more by disregarding the justice of the nobles' request. He had immediately suspected what his adversaries were up to and now he intended to forestall them with a bold move. In his reply to the nobles, he declared that he fully agreed with the citizens that the troops should be disbanded, and he threw all blame for the disorders on the court of Madrid because it had decided not to send him the money he needed to pay the soldiers. Finally, he himself proposed that an ambassador be sent to the court. He was sure that, in this way, he would be able to manipulate the selection of the ambassador and have someone chosen who was favorable to him, thus averting all danger to his position.

But the Neapolitan nobles needed no lessons from the Duke in the art of politics. They thanked him very graciously for his authorization to send an ambassador, whom they proceeded to select with the greatest secrecy.

Their choice was Father Lawrence of Brindisi, a happy selection, because the Saint, having been born in Brindisi, was a subject of the King of Spain, as they themselves were. He was also a diplomat, and had already given proof of his undoubted ability. Then, too, he had great prestige, for Philip III and the Queen held no one perhaps in higher esteem. Finally, his evident holiness rendered him eminently acceptable to the people of Naples, who, during his stay among them, had surrounded him with affection and enthusiastic veneration.

While Osuna was on the alert to find out the name of the chosen ambassador, the nobles, in strictest secrecy and with great circumspection, hastened to obtain permission from the Cardinal Protector and the General of the Order for Father Lawrence to act as their envoy, and when the required documents arrived, they got the guardian of the Immaculate Conception friary in Naples to summon Father Lawrence, who was then in Caserta and completely unaware of the new task that lay ahead of him. By late evening of October 1, the Saint was back again in Naples, where a score of nobles were waiting in the friary to outline their plan. When he pointed out the serious difficulties which he foresaw, they begged him not to refuse. To persuade him, they invoked the glory of God and the good of the Church and of souls. They pointed out that it was a question of averting a general uprising and unspeakable suffering among the oppressed people of the kingdom. Nevertheless, although he was fully aware of the gravity of the situation, Father Lawrence was not in any way disposed to undertake the task and gave in only when he was presented with the letters of obedience from

149

the Cardinal and the General, for then he knew that
the mission was the will of God for him.

That same night, travelling on horseback and disguised
as a Walloon soldier, he left Naples and climbed the
slopes of Mount Somma, from whence, on the following night, he rode down to the Capuchin friary at Torre
del Greco. These precautions were necessary because
Osuna had succeeded in finding out that Father Lawrence was the ambassador and had given his agents
orders to stop and even kill him if necessary. Orders
had also been issued to the crews of two fast feluccas to
patrol the coastline and detain the ambassador, should
he happen to choose the sea route.

After spending a few days at Torre del Greco waiting
for some confreres who were to join him, Father Lawrence braved the elements and the Duke's anger by
putting out to sea on a black wind-torn night. He
landed at Terracina in the papal states and went on to
Rome, where, without pausing to speak to anyone, he
once more took to the sea and eluded the merciless
pursuit of Osuna's feluccas. On October 25 he reached
Genoa safely just ahead of the Duke's ships. There,
learning that other enemy ships lay in wait for him in
the Gulf of Lyons, he decided not to put to sea again
except in a large vessel which would offer better protection against the attacks of his enemies. But the con-
sequent delay was fatal because Osuna, furiously
threatening the direst revenge, had wrung from the
Cardinal Protector and the procurator of the Capuchins
a counter command forbidding Father Lawrence to
continue his journey. This new document reached him
just as he was about to embark, and he had no choice
but to obey.

In Lisbon

When news of what had happened at Genoa reached Naples, the nobles were thrown into consternation while the Duke, now sure that he again held the whip hand, began to deal more severely than ever with his adversaries, among whom he now counted the Capuchins. At the same time, in order to offset any bad reports that might have reached the court at Madrid, he had a group of his supporters prepare letters praising his administration highly and asking that he be reconfirmed in office. However, this is not the place to record all the ruses and tricks he used to succeed in his plan. Suffice it to say that despite his scheming and the support of his friends at the court, many alarming details did eventually penetrate the thick barrier of censorship which had been erected to prevent the King from hearing about events in Naples. For his part, Father Lawrence succeeded in getting some letters delivered to the King, while a Neapolitan nobleman who had suffered greatly at Osuna's hands eluded the tyrant's vigilance and fled to Spain, where he made new, very grave, and very compromising accusations regarding the government of Naples. At the same time, in Madrid, Osuna's patron, the Duke of Uceda, began to fall from favor, and Osuna's numerous enemies at court began to take the offensive. Thus it finally came about that Philip III ordered the viceroy to allow Father Lawrence to continue his journey to Spain.

On April 5, 1619, the Saint, accompanied by Brother Giammaria of Monteforte and Father Girolamo of Casalnuovo, left Genoa in a convoy of Venetian galleys. Despite a violent squall in the Gulf of Lyons, they

arrived safely at Barcelona, from whence they journeyed to Madrid. Here Father Lawrence received the
unwelcome news that the King had left for Lisbon to
attend the coronation of Philip IV as King of Portugal.
Without wasting any time, the Capuchin set out once
more and on May 25 he caught up with the royal party
near the town of Almeda. Since there was no Capuchin
friary in the town, he was welcomed as a house guest
by Don Pedro de Toledo, the Marquis of Villafranca
del Bierzo, who, as an influential member of the King's
retinue, was quickly able to get the Saint an audience
with Philip III. Thus, on the day after his arrival,
Father Lawrence was received twice by the King, once
in the morning for a short presentation of his cre-
dentials, and again in the afternoon to explain his mission. This second audience lasted about three hours,
and from then on the doors of the royal household were
always open to the Saint. Needless to say, he made the
most of the opportunity to describe, with his usual force-
fulness, the crimes committed by Osuna. Not only did
he accuse the Duke before the King, but he also set out
to expose Osuna for what he was before the whole
court, by circulating a document vigorously denouncing
the viceroy's cruelty and oppression.

Although the stage seemed to be set for his swift downfall, Osuna and his supporters were not going to surrender without a fight. Recovering from their initial
shock, the Duke of Uceda and his party made a supreme effort to regain lost ground, while Osuna, with
undeniable skill and great shrewdness, gave them admirable support from Naples by sending gifts to the
King, the heir apparent, and various courtiers, by start-
ing a continuous stream of new recommendations for

his method of government, and by renewing his urgent requests that he be reconfirmed as viceroy. Furthermore, he was quick to profit by the revolt of the Bohemians against the Emperor and, taking advantage of the grave events that were already causing turmoil in Germany and the whole of Europe, he bragged about his foresight and made much of the services that his soldiers could render to the Catholic cause if they were sent to the north.

Meanwhile, Father Lawrence was finding it very difficult to hold his own against his adversaries and to ensure that the truth would win out. The King was hesitant to support him and, although he had the highest esteem for the Capuchin, he did not know what to believe, especially since the Holy See, fearing the Viceroy's anger, did not dare to lift a finger or say one word to cause his downfall. In short, the great expectations aroused by Father Lawrence's first audience with the King were fading swiftly. On one occasion, Philip, unable to hide his perplexity at the Saint's renewed accusations against Osuna, even went so far as to let it be clearly understood that he was not wholly persuaded of the truth of the Capuchin's statements. Father Lawrence reacted vigorously and in an unexpected way. Regarding himself more as the ambassador of God than as the envoy of the Neapolitans, he respectfully replied that he was as certain about the truth of his report as he was sure that he was to die soon and that the King, too, would be brought before God's tribunal within two years if he did not look to the welfare of his subjects. The Saint's prophecy struck fear into the king, a fear that was further increased when Father Lawrence did in fact fall sick at the end of June. However, the festivities held for the royal entry into Lisbon on June 29 and the solemn coronation of Philip IV on July 14, with all the formalities that preceded and followed it, soon distracted the King's mind from these forebodings.

The Saint's Death

However, Philip III received a rude awakening when he was informed that Father Lawrence was again seriously ill. As a matter of fact, the Saint's condition had been daily growing worse. The fatigue of his long journey, although he had borne it courageously, and the oppressive summer heat, had sapped the last remnants of his strength. During the latter part of June he had contracted dysentery. At first it had seemed that he would easily shake off this disease, yet, on the contrary, he had grown steadily worse until finally, upon the advice and almost the command of his companions and of Don Pedro de Toledo, he had stopped saying Mass. As he lay ill, growing weaker every day, a great number of people who knew and esteemed him came to see him, and the King, when informed of the Saint's illness, sent him his personal physicians and demanded a daily report of his progress.

Father Lawrence knew from the beginning that he was going to die, although everyone else was optimistic about his being cured. To those who spoke of a quick recovery he replied silently by looking upward and pointing toward heaven. Even before he had fallen ill, he had made several references to his approaching death; and now, lost in ever deepening recollection, he calmly awaited the end.

As death approached, he first spoke gratefully of

154

all those he had held dearest during his life; then he received the last rites of the Church with great devotion in the presence of many noblemen. Finally, death came to him peacefully on the afternoon of July 22, 1619. The mourning that followed was deep and sincere both on the part of the King and the heir apparent as well as on the part of Don Pedro and a multitude of others.

Don Pedro, who had received the Saint as a guest, provided for the embalming of his body, and the King, suspecting poison, sent his doctors to be present at the examination of the vital organs. No internal lesion was found, yet a grave suspicion of poisoning has remained even to the present day. When the embalming was finished, Don Pedro, to avoid having the Saint's body taken away from him, got permission from the King and the Archbishop of Lisbon to transport it quickly and secretly to his domain of Villafranca del Bierzo in Galicia. There the saintly remains were welcomed with holy joy rather than with mourning. The Saint's body was laid to rest in the church of the convent of Franciscan Sisters which had been founded by the Marquis' own daughter, and before long miracles began to happen at the tomb.

Osuna's Downfall

From his deathbed during the last hours of his life, Father Lawrence had sent Philip III a final warning and a final exhortation to have justice done to his oppressed subjects. Not content with this, the Saint had entrusted to the Marquis a sealed letter for Philip in which, as was later learned, he summoned both the King and Pope Paul V to appear before God's tribunal

155

within two years, the former to account for having failed to fulfill his grave obligations, and the latter to answer for his cowardice in not intervening to relieve the sufferings of the Neapolitans and to remove the dangers, both spiritual and material, that threatened them.

However, although this message increased his uneasiness, Philip III once more allowed his conscience to be lulled to sleep by Osuna's supporters, with the result that the Neapolitans' cause seemed irrevocably lost. Yet when Philip set out on his return journey after the heat of the summer had passed, he was surprised to find himself suffering from serious indispositions, and the memory of the Saint's threatening prophecy rose vividly before him. In addition, a religious who had heard the Saint's last words kept the memory of them alive in Philip's mind.

Upon his return to Madrid at the end of December, 1619, Philip III, gravely disquieted, set about having Osuna recalled. But getting the Duke to leave Naples was not easy. His successor as viceroy, Cardinal Borgia, succeeded in wresting from him the reins of government only by using a stratagem and only after the Duke, with the help of his supporters, had almost started a revolution. When Osuna finally did return to Spain, far from being accused of his crimes or put on trial, he was warmly welcomed by the King, and he went swaggering around Madrid, making no secret of his intention to return to Naples.

Certainly this was not the justice that Father Lawrence had called for on behalf of the Neapolitans. During his earthly life, the Saint had never favored compromise, nor did he change after his death. On January

28, 1621, Pope Paul V had been called to render an account before God's tribunal, and two months later, on March 31, Philip III was summoned to his reckoning, too—all less than two years after the Saint's death. While divine justice dealt inexorably with the King and the Pope, human justice was no less inexorable with Osuna. The new king, Philip IV, resolutely put him on trial, and on September 25, 1624, he died a lonely prisoner in the castle of Almeda.

The Neapolitans did not forget Father Lawrence's work and sacrifices, for on February 20, 1788, five years after his beatification, they included him among the patrons of their city. Thus was concluded the life work of this Saint who, despite his ardent longing for peace and recollection, had known only continuous war during his life—war by word against evil and error, war on the battlefield against the enemies of the Faith and Christian civilization, war side by side with the oppressed for the triumph of justice and right, war with the pen for the triumph of truth and the Catholic Church.

Chapter XI

The Doctor of the Church

EVEN before the Duke of Osuna's downfall, divine justice had begun to take a nobler and more solemn revenge on him than human justice was going to exact. While his star was rapidly falling and growing dim, the Saint's was rising and shining even more brightly with each passing day. The reputation for sanctity which had followed Father Lawrence during his life increased rapidly after his death. Everywhere so many graces and miracles were granted at the invocation of his name and the touch of his relics that, in 1624, while Osuna was sadly ending his days in a dungeon, Father Lawrence's *Processes of Canonization* were being introduced.

The Minister General had decided to take this step in view of the numerous extraordinary events which he himself had been able to verify during his visitation of the provinces of Spain and France. With the generous and enthusiastic support of Duke Maximilian of Bavaria, the Minister General had had no difficulty in surmounting all obstacles and in obtaining the needed permissions from Rome. During the course of the year 1625, the *Informative Processes* from Munich, Genoa, Verona, Bassano, Milan, Naples, Albenga and Vicenza had been furnished. But even before these processes

161

had been completed, the number of graces obtained through Father Lawrence's intercession and the continued growth of devotion to him had already decided the superiors of the Order and the Duke of Bavaria to ask the Holy See to introduce the *Apostolic Processes*. Everything pointed to a quick and successful development of the cause of beatification, but then Pope Urban VIII issued his famous decrees forbidding the introduction of causes earlier than fifty years after the death of the candidates.

Hence Father Lawrence's cause had to be laid aside, and nothing was attempted until 1673. Even then no great progress was possible because of new, more rigid and more complex norms regulating the procedure for canonization. Besides, during the second half of the seventeenth century and the first twenty years of the eighteenth, the popes were all rather reluctant to raise new saints to the honors of the altar. Consequently it was not until 1724 that the Capuchin's cause was taken up again with any enthusiasm. From 1724 to 1734 his writings were examined but it was only in May, 1761, that the ante-preparatory Congregation began to investigate the heroic nature of his virtues. The Bull of beatification was finally issued on May 23, 1783, and on June 1 of that year the solemn ceremony took place in the Vatican Basilica.

New miracles obtained through Blessed Lawrence's intercession led the Capuchin Superiors to ask that he be canonized. But unfortunately his cause was again interrupted, this time by the unhappy political and religious events and the social upheavals that led to the triumph of the French Revolution, to the persecution of the Church and the renewed suppression of the religious

162

orders. Almost a whole century was to pass before the great Pontiff, Leo XIII, elevated Father Lawrence to the supreme glory of the altars on December 8, 1881.

O Doctor Optime!

Although the name of Lawrence of Brindisi now shone like a bright star in the firmament of the Church's purest and holiest souls, one thing more was needed to complete the great joy of his fellow Capuchins. They had never been content to regard their illustrious brother solely as a great saint and an outstanding example of the Christian and religious life but had always thought of him in addition as a great teacher of the sacred sciences. All those who had known him in life had never ceased to praise his keenness of mind and the breadth and profundity of his knowledge. Later his biographers echoed these praises, thereby passing them on to new generations, while down through the centuries, artists had loved to depict the Saint engaged in writing his voluminous works.

It is true that very few scholars have had the opportunity or the ability to study his manuscripts and to plumb their depths. Yet those who have analyzed his work have been amazed at his genius, and one of them, a Cardinal, did not hesitate to say that Father Lawrence deserved to be counted among the Doctors of the Church.[1] Finally, in the Bull of canonization, Leo XIII was unstinting in his praise of the Saint's soaring

[1] Hieronymus a Fellette, O.F.M.Cap., *De S. Laurentii a Brundusio Ordinis Minorum Capuccinorum activitate apostolica ac operibus testimoniorum elenchus,* Venetiis, 1937, p. 217.

163

mind and teaching apostolate, while Pius XI later called him "a great luminary of science and sanctity." [2]

The desire for a complete knowledge of the Saint's works inspired many to undertake the monumental task of editing them. A special commission was even formed by a Minister General for this purpose but the immensity of the labor involved and the intrinsic difficulties of the project discouraged even the most selfless workers. Finally, in 1926, Father Vigilio of Valstagna, the minister provincial of Venice, set up a commission composed of priests from his province. This commission, first under Father Vigilio's personal direction and then under Father Angelico of Enego, resolutely set to work on their gigantic project and brought it to a successful close by publishing the ten volumes of the Saint's works in fifteen large, beautifully printed tomes which now form the fairest and most convincing monument to Lawrence of Brindisi's intellectual eminence and to the wide sweep of his knowledge.

In closing the Laurentian week held in Rome from May 8 to May 15, 1949, the late Cardinal Adeodato Piazza, with his usual skill and insight, developed the theme, *St. Lawrence of Brindisi, "vir apostolicus."* At the end of his speech, he expressed the unanimous sentiments of the eminent scholars who had taken part in the series of studies when he said: "But, with due reservation and submission, we believe that Lawrence of Brindisi still lacks one honor that should be his, namely, his being proclaimed a Doctor of the Universal Church. Of the three conditions required by Benedict XIV's classical norm—canonized sanctity; a large body of outstanding orthodox doctrine; and official recogni-

[2] *Ibid.*, p. 64.

tion by the Church's supreme authority—of these three conditions, St. Lawrence seems to lack only the last. The recent publication of his works in a critically perfect edition shows that his teaching is so vast and complete that it embraces almost all the sacred sciences, that his thought is marvellously in tune with the teaching and tradition of the Catholic Church, and that, while he is often ingenious and original in the presentation and development of problems and in the interpretation of the sacred texts, his words are always palpably seasoned with the unction of the Holy Spirit. Hence it only remains for us to hope that an official examination, authorized and guided by the competent authorities, will confirm our private opinions, and will soon give Christians the joy of being able to invoke Lawrence of Brindisi under the title of 'Excellent Doctor, light of Holy Church.' " [3]

On March 19, 1959, in the Apostolic Letter, *Celsitudo ex humilitate,* His Holiness Pope John XXIII granted the wish of the scholars and fulfilled the centuries-old desire of the Capuchins by placing the aureola of a Doctor on St. Lawrence's head, thereby establishing a new claim to our devotion and gratitude.

[3] *S. Lorenzo da Brindisi. Studi,* Vol. I of *Miscellanea Laurentiana,* Padova, 1951, p. 244s.

A NOTE ON THE TYPE

IN WHICH THIS BOOK IS SET

This book is set in Times Roman, a Linotype face created by Stanley Morrison, world-famous typographical authority. It was designed for the London *Times,* which demanded a type face that should be clear and legible, precise but not mechanical, having a high letter but not condensed, of a "color" suitable for any paper or printing process, with character but not with annoying characteristics. The clear, open characters of Times Roman are the secret of its clear printing on any paper, whether it be on the coarsest of newsprint or the finest coated paper. This book was composed and printed by the Wickersham Printing Company of Lancaster, Pa., and bound by Moore and Company of Baltimore. Typography and design are by Howard N. King.